MORE THAN A  the Other Side of the Door

Judy L. Gates

To My Dear Friend
Cathy Audrey
You have encouraged
and inspired me this
past 21 years. I am
always grateful for
our friendship.
Love Always
Judy Gates

What is the Point?

Why I am writing a book is really beyond me, and certainly way beyond my capabilities. I have pondered why writing about something that I can effectively do in a coma could be so difficult. After all I am completely entertaining and should have the attention of everyone who is in ear shot. I have been told I know everything or am a "know it all" or some such statement by so many individuals of every rank that it must be true!

So what is the purpose? Why have I gathered a snippet of my life stories into what will likely resemble a tiny bathroom reader or short novel? It is, of course, because I think they are fascinating, not only due to their significance to me, but because of the point of view from which one will see and perhaps comprehend the daily life of a nurse. That is no small task my friends.

You see nursing and healthcare are not the reflection of the faux documentary fare seen every day on the television set in your home. The entertainment industry has captured some of the character of the healthcare profession, but has not adequately reflected the heart of a "die hard" nurse. Shows reflect the interactions and emotions from one side, but never really identify what led to those encounters in the first place. You see nursing is much more than a job. This book will give you a glimpse of what it is like from my view, the other side of the door.

Where to Begin?

I think I will start at the end of my last career as it were and work my way back from there. "Tell them that where ever they land it will be wonderful" she declared from her fine, over padded desk chair. Her position recently elevated, her view had been perhaps slightly skewed as the rest of us sat around with upset stomachs eating bottles of antacids over the course of the day. Since news of the reorganization had reached the lower ranks, no one felt secure in the least. Twenty three days, that's how long since the announcement that our second in command had been dethroned. The newly appointed leaders sat in closed door meetings for hours each day without a hint of resolution.

Healthcare is one of those industries that most feel is untouchable, even in the darkest times. It is true, people are terminal beings, and they will eventually find themselves in the inner sanctum of some medical institution, whether it is a clinic, hospital or a morgue. Personally, I am not sure which service I would prefer some days. That being said, healthcare is a necessary commodity. And working for a major multi-state healthcare organization certainly provides diverse opportunity for providing enhanced patient care. But the direction of this conversation is likely not the least bit interesting to you the poor reader suffering through this pre-loque.

Today, corporate healthcare has become one large sea of cubicles, full of average Joe's waiting to see whose number is up. Who knew it would be me. So like every codependent caregiver, I felt that to sit and dawdle while looking for my next great adventure was truly a waste of time. That is where this whole book writing thing began. I instead have chosen to finish a story 35 41 years in the making. That's right it only took an additional SIX years to complete.

What is the deal with Healthcare Anyway?

The media is full of news about nursing

shortages, nursing burnout, patient safety issues and then there is the great lawsuit mania. You cannot begin to watch television or read a magazine without some law firm advertising their services for medical malpractice. "It is always someone's fault" you or your loved one develops a complication or passes away. As much as they would like you to believe that, the truth is many things are simply out of the hands of the medical professionals'. They try the latest measures to treat and to heal but despite those efforts they cannot. AND you were given the extensive list of risks before you begged them to try anyway.

We are a society that has been taught to blame all of our defects and shortcomings on others and it has crossed over into the healthcare arena. While your momma might have made you clean your plate not one nurse has forced you to eat doughnuts, smoke cigarettes, drink alcohol, disregard your diabetes, fail to keep your annual appointments or ignore their heart problems. Not one! And not one nurse has figured out how to prevent the ultimate end, death. It comes for us all! The bell will toll and the fat lady is already warming up.

Then there is the news about the nursing crisis. Are we having a nursing shortage? Perhaps, if we are to use today's staffing expectations of a one to four patient ratio, even if that may not be the right balance. Are patients in more danger today than they were twenty years ago? Absolutely! Medicine is attempting to care for illnesses they would not even have treated in the past. They are administering medications and treatments that have a whole set of potential complications of their own. The patients we see today would have passed away one hundred percent of the time twenty years ago from things with which we now have success.

Can we prevent a bad outcome even if there is one nurse to one patient? Maybe. Can bad things happen even if everything is done right? Certainly! Can good things happen even when things are done wrong? Yes! While we can't always explain the outcomes, what is certain is this; eventually it is time for each of us to go. The best medical evidence suggests that everyone dies despite all of our best work. Bummer, right?

As for burnout, well if you had to walk into a room and get yelled at, or watch a life end, or see someone abused every ten minutes day after day it can happen to anyone. The answer for those who cannot find a way to debrief or unwind is that they may need to move into a different area with a different patient population, find different patient to nurse ratios or move to another sector of healthcare entirely. Fast food or auto repair may be better settings for that individual who has lost their coping skills altogether. I think it comes most often as the result of caregiver exhaustion, their emotions constantly "on duty". It is a combination of the extreme roller coaster ride stuck in the loop that takes its toll. Much like that amusement park ride, the first three times on the roller coaster are great. The fourth or fifth time not so much!

And of course nurses do not take care of themselves, me included. They don't get rest, exercise, eat well or have adequate social time with friends or family. These same habits affect professional and lay community caregivers alike. Sometimes you have to move on or change, and admit you need help, rest, time off. Plain and simple, we are all human, more alike than unalike. When situations are tough, putting self first seems impossible, yet it is critical to wellbeing and survival in the nursing profession.

As for that shortage, in the seventies and eighties it was often two registered nurses, one or two nursing assistants and a unit secretary for an entire floor of sixty or more patients. The ratios that drive the criticism of a shortage are significantly different today with a nurse and an assistant or practical nurse for five to ten patients. Intensive care units used to have three or four patients to one nurse and now grumbling can be heard if they have two or three patients. Not to be unsympathetic, it is back to the fact that we have patients critically ill that fifteen years ago would not even be given the opportunity to have extreme measures taken. We have developed the art of keeping people alive longer, like it or not, and this creates a more complex work environment.

So what is the truth about this profession that has grabbed the headlines of Reader's Digest to the Wall Street Journal? What is it that drives a nurse to come in day after day? It is the complexity of the human heart. It is a profession of caring, even in the gut wrenching face of death. It is a profession of education, where patients are taught that they have much control over their health and are indeed often responsible for their condition. It is a profession of giving, where a nurse goes the extra mile to see that you are fed, medicated, and have a clean bed to mend in. It is a profession of patience, where nurses smile, listen, problem solve and serve the many visitors that are in the room each day. It is a profession of active listening, to patients who yell, tease, cry, laugh, grieve and reminisce. It is a profession that changes you every day as you observe how families deal with each life situation. It is a profession where ninety-nine point nine percent of the nurses are sincere and compassionate.

It is a profession that goes home with you. Nursing is a twenty-four hour a day business. What doesn't get resolved at work can often keep you up at night. Not the physical details like paperwork, politics and patient attitude, though they may delay your ability to rest, but it is the emotions of those you meet each day. People finding out they are going to die, have lost an unborn child or are sick and going to be out of work. The complex families filled with tears, anxiety or anger. There is a certain amount that we can detach from, but some things get through the armor. That's when you know that you are in the toughest job. It is also a job that can bring with it the greatest rewards; hugs, thanks, laughs and warm smiles. It is more than a job. It is all those things that happen on the other side of the door that draws us in. Each of us has a story how we find our way into this profession, this is mine.

> **"Nobody who ever gave his best**
>
> **regretted it."** *George Halas*

WHERE IT ALL BEGAN

I might have figured out that my destiny was nursing. Not everybody would enjoy caring for sick, vomiting, injured, unstable or mentally challenged people. Of course having experienced all of these things I feel very comfortable in this environment. Everyday has been an adventure. I suppose it all started with my first exposure to medicine. It was late at night and it was winter, in the Midwest, and yes, there was snow. As a parent, just when you think you are done for the night, the kids are in bed and your favorite show is on, you hear a noise. Great, someone is up. You walk down the hall to see your slender, tall, long legged 2-year old standing on the bathroom counter looking for more "candy". You notice the "candy" jar is empty and that it is clearly labeled orange flavored chewable aspirin. Not seeing any pills on the floor you assume there is only one place they could be and you know there is only one way to get them out, the emergency room.

As the car crept out the driveway and slid down the street, we had quite a ride with all the ice and those nifty, bald 1962 tires. When we finally arrived at the hospital, the waiting room was crowded. They listened to our story and decided they needed to get us right in. Large amounts of aspirin are known to cause problems such as bleeding. The only solution was to pump the stomach and watch the tot overnight. After a lot of thrashing, screaming and bodily harm to the staff the deed was done and we were on our way to the hospital room. Fortunately sleep came quickly seeing as the cute little girl was exhausted from all that fighting. When morning came we got to go home. It may be of interest for you to know that I was the little darling who ingested the aspirin while my parents were attempting to have a little quiet time before bed. They gave that up.

I must have been seriously impressed with the experience because it was not long after that I saw and demanded a doctor's kit. It was the one that looked like a lunchbox but when you opened it, it contained a little doctor's office, a nurse and a doctor. I quickly resolved to cure any and all family members, pets and toys. No one was safe from a thorough exam by Dr. Feelgood and Nurse Happy. And so my career began.

I have found throughout the years that experience and knowledge are critical in providing great care. I failed to realize that I did not always have to have firsthand experience to gain that knowledge. Before the age of ten I would have stitches to my head for a cut received while racing through the house with my sister chasing me, have regular bouts of strep throat, have injured my ear drum while poking it with a pick-up stick and a broken arm from a disastrous attempt to use a footsie. What did I learn from all of this? Never run in the house, don't poke things in your ears and when you have not mastered walking without falling you should not try to skip and jump a rope at the same time. All this would provide a great foundation for the lifetime of learning I was about to receive.

I continued my path of 'self-directed studies'

in medicine. I was totally into biology and the whole life process by the seventh grade. It was a pivotal time in our country, war was going on and people were protesting. It may have been the 70's but I won't own up to it though I do recall wearing floral print blue jeans and knee high boots. Anyway, I really wanted to grasp the life process completely. Part of life is the necessity for food. Now my biology teacher was attempting to help us understand the natural process of survival of the fittest, the circle of life so to speak. So of course she provided the traditional snake versus mouse scenario. There sat this snake in his glass house waiting for a meal. Our job was to feed it. I volunteered so that I could experience the satisfaction of providing sustenance to our pet snake. As I held the little mouse by its' tail and prepared to place it in the snake pit, it curled up and bit me clean through the end of my finger. Try to explain to the

Pentagon that your dad needs to leave work because your science project has just attacked, and it wasn't even the dangerous one. It took a long time for him to live that one down.

As soon as I turned fourteen I was able to apply for a candy striper position. No pay just free meals. Hmmmm, hospital food as a reward. That likely only works for teenagers! It would be during this time that I would solidify my desire to be a nurse and really begin to see the more serious side of medicine. Oh, there would be the fun stuff, like feeding cute babies and sitting on the bathroom floor for hours trying to convince a stool-holding child to poop. I also enjoyed spending time listening to life stories from the geriatric patients. There would also be some very sad events such as the day I arrived to find a nice gentleman gone who had been there two days before. He had passed away, alone. I had not been able to come back as I had promised and I have always regretted not being there for him. I began to realize early that everyone does not have a special someone to be there and not everyone goes home in a car. Big lessons learned young.

There are rewards greater than any single negative thing I have ever thought of that makes this job great. It is the smile from a patient, a hug from a family member or the ability to hold a hand of someone who is afraid and alone. There is the laughter and tears, anger and passion. And my own silly or painful life events have provided me the ability to have some compassion and empathy for those who have had to endure. At that young age I had experienced lots of personal injury and illness. I learned from those I met dealing with critical things about the value of life, time, family and hope.

"You've got to think about 'big things'

while you're doing small things, So that all

the small things go in the right direction."

Alvin Toffler

STORIES FROM THE KITCHEN AND MORE

As time passed I had broken three more bones, had surgery and quit my first round of college. So here it is. When I left home the first time I enrolled in the nursing program, of course. This made my parents very happy. Now the one thing I had enjoyed all through my school years was my clarinet and the marching band. I was a 4-H medal winner after all. Of course we all got a medal, but it was a medal just the same. During nursing program orientation I was told that if I wanted to be in the marching band I was in the wrong place. I was either a nursing student 100% or not at all. Fair enough. I left orientation and registered for general classes, giving up nursing school. I can honestly say that it was a huge mistake but at the time it seemed logical! I was after all seventeen. My parents were not excited about the decision and the future of their financial investment. I accomplished nothing during the following year and a half, carrying a stellar 1.8 grade point average. In case you are reading this and you are young, you should know that the lower the number the lower your grade. In other words, I stunk.

It was after I dropped out of college that I went back to a hospital kitchen job. I had worked in the kitchen throughout high school and had fond memories of the smell of burnt bacon, and slightly less fond memories of steam tables with liver and fish. The kitchen or food service department was not a job for patient contact. It was however a great time to learn how to cook for the masses and discover the fun of water play in the sub-zero South Dakota winters. For those of you who have never gone outside with wet cloths in 20 below weather, it is good to know that your clothes freeze stiff making it difficult to bend and for that fact move. Water fights were a common event while cleaning the dishes.

This particular hospital was a Catholic hospital and also a teaching hospital in the Midwest. It was part of our job to help feed the 500 or so patients as well as the doctors when they would have special events. I was exposed to cooking things like prime rib, chicken or the ever-famous rocky mountain oysters (these oysters are not found in the water but on the under carriage of an angry, now second tenor bull). We would have to prepare these feasts for as many as 300. I never had my hands in so much slimy stuff, but the exposure to things that look gross and squish would come in handy later.

Patient trays are prepared on a tray line, which equates to a factory conveyor belt only with more 'aromas'. Most people have certain foods they don't like, but when placed on a steam table the smell of some things rising up to your face is enough to make you achieve Olympic record time on your way to the loo. I know liver won me more gold medals than Mark Spitz ever dreamed of. And fish, well that's another story all together.

A regular occurrence in the Midwest is "the blizzard". In this community it may mean days with road closures. For those of us who lived close to a snow route (a plowed road) it meant getting to the hospital and staying until others could come. One winter I was there for three days with two other regular kitchen staff and a dozen nuns. There was a lot of toast and cold cereal served for breakfast followed by cold sandwiches for lunch. As it turns out, though they were nice, the nuns were not very creative in the kitchen. Food Service did not score high points for patient satisfaction during those times but we tried. I gleaned flexibility and creativity are must have essential tools, ones I am perfecting to this day.

"Ordinary people with commitment can make an extraordinary impact on their world."

John C. Maxwell

A STEP CLOSER TO NURSING

My life training would continue as a unit secretary on the medical floors. I will pause to say that to this day I love unit secretaries! Talk about a tough job. Tons of people demanding to know where someone is, where their chart is, where the test results are and what you intend to do about it all. I remember in one hospital the charts were labeled with a specific colored tape selected by the physician. This was supposed to make it easier for them to find their patients charts. Well, we ran out of the shade of pink used by a particular surgeon. He reported he was therefore unable to find his charts! He came unglued, and when we explained that we were out of his tape and the chart was in its right place with a different shade of pink, he bellowed, "Well how am I supposed to find my charts?" I could have held my tongue, but why. "Reading is something that you could try," I told him. I turned around and prayed he would be too shocked to retaliate. He stood there staring for what seemed like hours. I was fortunate, this time he walked away. To this day I still encourage physicians to read.

In the 70's and 80's most patients could walk

around and care for themselves. Those who couldn't were either in the intensive care or the nursing home. At night there may be one registered nurse, one or two licensed practical nurses and an aide plus the secretary for up to sixty patients. It was rare that anything serious happened on the regular floors but every once in a while we would get some excitement. When the excitement happened, the secretary was fully included in the action.

I remember a new nurse who was covering a surgical patient. The patient had some abdominal surgery earlier that day and had returned to the floor. The nurse kept complaining that every time she walked by the room the patient was scratching the incision under the sheets. She would wake the patient up (clue number one) and tell them to stop, but this to no avail. As she is telling this to us, we all have the same idea. We all ran to the room, threw back the sheets and there were the patients' intestines crawling around on top of the abdomen. The nurse was terrified at the sight of a dehisced (open) incision, but with a little normal saline and a quick call to the physician the patient was back in the operating room and as good as new by morning. It was from this I learned to always expect the unexpected (but usually not intestines).

Another key concern for those of us working in the hospital was patients on oxygen who also smoked, that would be most of them on the respiratory floor. In the good old days, there were no restrictions on smoking in the hospital. So a patient admitted with COPD or chronic obstructive pulmonary disease or emphysema would get a breathing treatment, have oxygen on and then lite up the old stogy.......while their oxygen was on. At this point visions of explosions like those seen in the movies should come to mind. Over the years we learned to encourage and eventually restrict smoking in hospitals. This caused nurses to breathe easier, no pun intended.

My next move was to the acute care psychiatric unit, as an employee. Many of the patients in the psych unit were there for depression and other mental states that could be in part or full related to a failure to achieve or motivate while the rest were genuinely ill. There were some interesting situations that have always remained with me. In some ways they may sound like One Flew Over The Cuckoos Nest but in others they revealed the state of the human mind in crisis. And just between you and me I would say many of my friends and family are not far removed from the mental health patients I worked with. Seriously! Ooops, 'Love you, mean it!'

My first observation was that some of the staff closely assimilated the behavior of some of the patients. And I came to find out that one of the staff had actually been a patient and hid this information from the personnel department during the hiring process. I asked for my own set of keys during the first orientation day just to be sure I would have a quick exit should the patients or staff have a hostile event.

One dear lady suffered from manic depression. She came in deeply depressed but by the third day had converted to her happy manic side. This apparently occurred during her shower, an experience I certainly have never had. Before she could be stopped she was dancing on the tables free as a bird and singing with only her towel flowing behind. While in itself this may not be a sound state of mind, there was something to be said for singing and dancing. We finally convinced her to at least get dressed before her next performance.

Then there was Daniel, a very handsome man who came in regularly for schizophrenia. He had the most pleasant face. He would be talking to or feel he was Jesus. He was Jesus with an attitude off medication and the most rational, gentle man on medication. It was challenging to decide what would cause him to stop taking his medication which would always set off the hallucinations. Then I remembered, "I am in healthcare" and one thing I know is that most healthcare complications are the result of some form of noncompliance or rebellion. For Daniel, when he was mad he would get revenge by stopping his medication. Not so sure how well that really worked for him.

And no story would be complete without at least one life threatening episode. The general public does not understand that nurses risk their lives every day whether the threat comes from a patient, visitor or peer. In the behavioral health unit there were rules to be followed especially in the lock up unit. The primary rule being no smoking during activities. It was my job to enforce that rule. Oh joy. Well, one man was not too pleased with that rule and decided to take it out on the therapist. He had requested cigarettes for the umpteenth time and I told him "No you cannot smoke during activities. You know this as you are here often and the rules have not changed".

So he walked over and stood behind the therapist, grabbed him around the neck and attempted to choke him to death while staring at me. A "Code Man" was called. This meant every man working in the hospital should race to the seventh floor and hold down the crazy guy. They were able to pry him loose and place him in isolation until his medication kicked in. Mac, the therapist, wanted to know what took so long as I guess when you are being strangled two minutes seems long. Who knew? Once we completely discussed that issue he wanted to know why he choked him and not me. I was not sure I liked that question, but the fact was that the patient stated he would never hurt a woman. And while that may seem sexist, I was all for it.

It would be another patient, "Rose", that would change my whole perspective on the power of the spoken word and human actions. It impacts every patient care interaction I have to this day. She was a young gal, married with a lovely son. She had somehow slipped into a deep depression. She would simply sit and stare or shuffle in a line back and forth. A catatonic state was what the medical record stated. She would not care for herself or feed herself. Doctors had done a number of tests to see if there was some other cause but found nothing. Nurses tried everything from kindness to harsh words. One nurse would even talk down to the patient while feeding her, insulting her by telling her she looked like a pig while letting the food drip down her face and onto her clothes. Cold, cruel behavior!

Numerous medications were tried for this gal with no change. As a last resort electric shock therapy was done several times. No changes were seen and the treatments were eventually held. Most of the staff took compassion on "Rose" and it would be one day while in the shower that her recovery would begin. There was something mystical about that shower room. The nurse giving her a shower was turning off the water when her hand slipped, honestly slipped, off the knob. The water instantly became cold and the patient yelled, "Turn it off". The nurse was shocked; these were her first words in four months. She told "Rose" she would turn off the water if she would talk and she agreed. And talk she did.

It would not be long before we started to find out about her problems at home that started the depression. But more important was the fact that she recalled every single word and action by every staff since the day she came in. She knew our names and who had done what. She had a particular dislike for the nurse who constantly talked down to her and let food drip on her face and clothes. Even in an apparent state of disconnect, she was completely aware of the events around her. A valuable lesson I still remember today. No matter what an individual's function or level of conscious appears to be, treat every patient as if they were fully present, able minded and making full eye contact.

"You have not lived today successfully unless you've done something for someone who can never repay you.'

John Bunyan

LET THE TRAINING BEGIN

It was while working in the psychiatric unit that I decided I needed to move on with getting some nursing education otherwise I was likely to be admitted, or committed. I felt as if I was the only one not in therapy. I was told by many I was repressed. Sure I was repressed to a degree, because I was holding back my true fear of patients, a co-worker and shock therapy. So here I began the next chapter. I had miserably underachieved at college the first go round, not really a lack of brains as much as a lack of effort. But I had since decided marching band was not a real priority. Fun, but not essential to my future. So I looked into school options and found a practical nursing program that would leave me with an LPN.

School was a gas, if you like tests, reading, working for no pay and days without sleep. I had a retired drill sergeant for a teacher, or at least that was our impression based on her "maneuvers" during our hospital clinical days. Each day we would arrive at clinical and were immediately ordered into a lineup for inspection. She made sure we looked spit-spot from the white shoes and white laces to the hair which she expected to be pulled back and snug. It was not at all unusual to have a classmate sent home for inadequate grooming. Her pet peeves were untrimmed nails and a poorly mitered corner of the hospital bed sheets. For the children under 30 reading this, bed sheets didn't used to have elastic. You lucky kids!!

Without fitted sheets we had to make them look just like the soldiers. You have seen the old Shirley Temple war time movies. It was just like that only no singing, dancing or happy ending. She would always remind us that the sheets should be so snug she would be able to bounce a dime on them. Her way of letting you know you had not achieved this goal would be to place the call light on in your patients' room. When you arrived you would find the patient in a chair and your sheets on the floor. One day a classmate went through six sets of sheets. She came crying into the break room. We did a tag team effort to distract the teacher long enough to help her make the bed. We had no guilt, after all this was linen not medication. We were successful thank God. And the patients were great at keeping the secret. I think it was all the crying or it could have been the fact that they just wanted to lay down!

Our favorite teacher was the anatomy and physiology teacher. She had a great sense of humor. One day we stuck the skeleton in the locker fully dressed. When she opened the locker to hang her coat she screamed so loud the entire office staff came racing down the hall to see what happened. The teacher laughed so hard she nearly wet her pants. She was the same teacher we walked out on for the last day of class. As she called roll, we said "here", we stood up and left. She started giggling, and as the last person was called they handed her a note with the address to the restaurant we would be at if she wanted to come. She did, and she was still laughing. Laughter is critical if you are in healthcare. Lesson learned.

It was during school that I survived my first tornado. We were listening to lecture while the weather was changing outside. The view was much more captivating than the monotone lecturing. As I was gazing at the brewing storm it became strangely calm when all of the sudden a tree blew straight over. In a split second we dove for cover in the hallway. When it was over we went outside to find trees down, electrical lines in the street, roofs gone and about three feet of water. As I drove home I saw a path of damage I would later find out had gone across the entire town. Amazingly no one was hurt. Lesson of the day; don't get out of your car if it is stuck in deep water with utility lines dangling on your windshield.

As with any program, there were the classmates that we were hoping would not survive. In fact there camc a point when we were wondering what they did to get in. One gal had no sense of anatomy. None. Zip!! This became flagrantly evident when she explained to her patient that she hoped she would be able to put the NG tube (that lovely tube they put in your nose) in the right place otherwise it might come straight out the other end. She was serious. It was her last day in the program. It is great and passionate nursing instructors that censor and expel those hopeful nurse want-to-bees who, if passed, would scare you straight into the morgue. If you love a nurse, be sure to thank the instructor who mentored them.

When you are in a nursing program, you are only allowed so many absences. If exceeded, you most often have to repeat the entire semester. I had planned on missing one day at the end of the program for a scheduled surgery. One week before however, my father had a massive heart attack. He had open-heart surgery and bypass. He survived to the ripe old age of 84 and did very well. That in itself is remarkable as bypass was an experimental procedure at the time. But back to me, this crisis caused a huge dilemma. I had to pick out a patient for my clinical the next day. I could not miss any time or I would have to repeat the semester. After a dozen phone calls and meeting with the physicians, it was clear my father was going to need surgery. So while he was in surgery I ran to the floor and picked out a patient.

Of course the other thing that happens in these high stress family situations is a sudden influx of houseguests all arriving in the wee hours and not a morsel of food in the house. A hundred years ago stores were not open late on Sundays or for that fact any night. You may not know, but 7-11 was named so because that was the operating hours of the store. It was the only place open. I walked in with a blank check from my mom, as this was the pre-debit era. They initially did not want to take this check. When I told him what happened that day, and cried, he put down his paper and went with me aisle by aisle to collect all the essential items. It wasn't much, but peanut butter and jelly with pudding cups which is not all bad at times like these. It was a very bright spot in a challenging day and reinforced my belief that there are still some nice people in the world; I am just not always sure where they are.

"One is not born into the world to do everything, but to do something."

Henry David Thoreau

The End of Silliness?

At the school for crippled children meals were typically taken in the cafeteria and served family style. Now I had a very traditional family table, rather Presbyterian or Baptist (depending on where we were stationed) in many ways. Conservative, quiet, controlled. We ate without much excitement. I had friends who I would visit from time to time with six children and a very unconventional set of parents. They had the anything goes type household. While I found a lot of their free living a bit "beyond" me, I found it a gas to eat meals with them and watch the milk spew across the table as someone cracked a funny. It would be something I enjoy to this day.

So it would be no surprise for my table at the school to get into trouble for being loud and silly. One night we (my dorm room of 8 and 9 year old girls) decided to wear our clothes inside out to dinner. Sounded perfectly wonderful to me! For hats we wore decorated diapers (unused of course). We strolled into the cafeteria like usual but were laughing so much that it was not long before we had everyone else giggling as well. The next thing we know the supervisor comes marching over and tells us to calm down. She already knew that wouldn't work, hadn't

yet, so she smiled and walked away. She would at

least be able to defend herself should a higher

authority complain.

You see, the very first night I worked at the

school I helped my four charges act out Dr. Seuss

stories in the dorm room. We were laughing and

making so much noise that she felt the need to check

on us. I was new after all. At the very moment she

opened the door I was wearing a little chair on my

head and standing on the bed. She scanned the room,

shook her head and closed the door. Over the years

that followed she never looked in again. And I still

love to act out Dr. Seuss!

Well I survived the practical nursing program

and passed my license exam at the exact same

moment our state decided to go RN (registered

nurses) only. Exact, got my license the very day the article hit the paper. Hundreds of nursing assistants and LPN's were laid off in hospitals across the state. The only jobs readily available were in the boonies (small towns without fast food or department stores). Two jobs really had the most appeal, one in a hospital between two Indian reservations and the other, which I took, at the state hospital for the mentally retarded (that's what it was called then). It was in a town of three thousand with four hundred and fifty of those residing at the state hospital.

I truly enjoy working with disabled children and adults even today. I had worked at a hospital and school for crippled children during my LPN program. Loved it! For my job at the state hospital I worked in the infirmary, which had a twelve-bed capacity. I was the only licensed nurse for the entire campus at night and as a new grad nurse I felt a little overwhelmed at times. Actually, terrified may best describe some days. It was one thing to try to treat individuals who might be able to tell me what was wrong, but these residents were not able to do that. I quickly learned I didn't know as much as my nursing board test scores said I did.

The residents ranged in age from eight years old to eighty-three years old. Every imaginable health diagnosis and developmental delay was represented. As a matter of fact, the only documented Native American twins with Down syndrome lived there. Government testing often happens at state facilities. It was while I worked there that the government approved the Hepatitis B vaccine series for testing. The employees of the state were voluntold for this and we in turn received the entire vaccine series in our rumps. We were sad to learn later that the injections are ineffective given in the backside and instead had to be given in the arm. Guess who had to have them again? That's right! While I no longer kicked and screamed as I did as a little girl, the thought did cross my mind. I hope you appreciate my sacrifice for mankind, I know your behind does.

To fill my spare time I worked part time on the local rural ambulance. The little hospital in town was good for cuts, bruises, baby deliveries and minor surgery but not ideal for serious injuries. Most of the folks we picked up were minor problems such as chest pain, someone ready to deliver or car accident victims with light trauma. Big problems had to be transported thirty-two miles to the bigger hospital up the road. One critical accident victim needed immediate surgery. We made the trip in eighteen minutes, which we attribute to straight, open highways and a miracle. My mother's reaction to this exciting tale was "At least you had a seatbelt on." I smiled. It is, after all, impossible to do resuscitation with a seatbelt on while you are alone in the back with the patient. It was always worth it to me.

"Deep awareness of the suffering of another coupled with the wish to relieve it."

The American Heritage Dictionary, 2009

HEALTHCARE ON STEROIDS

From this tiny town I moved to the big city. It was 1985. A million or more documented residents and probably that many undocumented was the recorded census when I arrived. More than one language spoken here and I was still working on my native tongue. As you can clearly see I have not made much progress. I worked through a nursing registry service traveling to nursing homes all over the city and finally landed at a primary care clinic job with an urgent care center. One of my favorite bofoos happened here as I strutted out to the waiting area and called "Jesus" (as in the Lord) back for his appointment, twice. The entire room broke out in laughter. I soon learned that the J's are pronounced like H's in Spanish. From that day forward the Lord has not been summoned from my waiting room.

I was later exonerated as a translation issue occurred with a Hispanic Nursing Assistant. When patients would come in she would ask the Spanish speaking patients or their parents how long they had had their symptoms such as the rash to their skin. Every time she asked they would laugh. Finally she asked one parent why they were laughing and she was told that the word she used for skin meant chicken skin. So for all the years she was in the U.S. she was asking patients how long they had the rash on their chicken skin. It was the word her mom had always used so she did not know another. She learned there were many slang or dialect variations in her own homeland that she had been unaware of. And her mother had never gone to school so likely was repeating from generations of poultry loving relatives. I took solace in knowing if it could happen to her, it could happen to anybody.

During this time a wonderful doctor who moonlit, as many of them do at the clinic, suggested I take a job at the county hospital. He told me I would love it, learn a ton and see unusual things. I took him at his word and obtained a position on the Pediatric floor, night shift, twelve hour shifts. I did see things I had never dreamed of, good and bad. I learned of the world of residents and interns and medical students all of which provided hours of fun and laughter for the nursing staff. Nerves make people easy targets and no one is more nervous than a medical student.

After a couple of years I decided to go back to school for my RN (Registered Nursing) degree. I applied at a few schools and decided on the community college route. Part of the reason was that the university would not transfer any of my previous education. As a matter of fact, they would not even consider my practical nursing education, as it was not a "real" school. So they based the final part of their decision on that first college experience, the one I failed. I would have to go to a community college for a semester and prove myself before I could apply at the university. Then it would take me four years to get my degree. Can you see dollar signs? Okay, community college it is.

I was ecstatic that they not only transferred my practical nursing studies but the couple of classes I had passed during "the dark years" as well. I worked full time and went to school full time. I don't remember sleeping at all but I do remember freaking out at regular intervals. I even remember nearly dying during my microbiology class. It's true. My lab partner routinely lit the burner with the flame under the gas tubing. My instructor would fly across the room to shut off the gas valve. I think I got a sympathetic passing grade in her class for the danger I endured. Well that and the neck brace from my car accident made me look particularly helpless. Scarier still to me was that this would-be arsonist was another nursing student who made the rest of us afraid for our lives.

Work carried on while I was at school and provided a necessary diversion. One of the things we loved to do to pass the time was think of ways to torture the doctors. It was always a great lot of fun to see how far we could push our new interns and residents. Usually, late at night, there is less to do as the procedures, tests and bulk of the physician rounds are done during the day. Residents and interns often were in the hospital two or three days at a time with call schedules and rounds. These long stretches were supplemented with a lecture or two, like they could stay awake. Tired, bleary eyed and likely malnourished they were easy targets especially in the dark. And before you get all sympathetic, they were perfectly willing to retaliate. And did, but this is my story.

Given the nature of the children in the intensive care, the residents often did not sleep and if they tried it was not good sleep. Nurses at night spent those quiet moments thinking of things to do to insight fear in those doing what they could not which was sleep. The easiest way to cause panic amongst the doctors was with a stat call to the intensive care for something serious like babies not breathing well or breathing too quickly. The more nervous or alarmed the nurse sounded the faster the doctor would run to the room.

Wiping the sleep out of their eyes they would try and focus on the monitors displaying no heartbeats or obscure numbers. They would shout out directions for tests or medicine. They would fuss with their stethoscopes trying to get them untangled from around their neck and into the ears. The staff would be standing back trying not to laugh. As soon as the doctor pulled back the little blankets they would know they had been had. They would find teddy bears or toy dolls in baby clothes with wires running here and there. It was almost too easy. Once the poor doctors heart slowed down they would usually laugh then head back for bed. Occasionally we would find one without a sense of humor. They were doomed of course. We felt it a necessary part of their training to include attitude adjustments, though this course would never appear on the official syllabus.

Another way to play with the residents and interns was to seal their doors with saran wrap or plastic, or place a well-endowed mannequin at the door. Once they receive those midnight calls and attempt to walk out the door for a trip to the loo, they would run smack into the plastic and bounce back or let out a nice shriek as an unexpected figure greeted them. Great fun to be sure. Can you imagine the list of ideas a dozen people can come up with at night, in the dark? The potential is endless. I am thinking of more things right now!

We had one nurse who felt that physicians often think of nurses as secretaries or servants. She felt completely committed to the work of changing that mindset to one of a professional-to-professional relationship. It was after all the 80's. The new residents always had a hard time finding things from floor to floor such as the charts or computers or supply rooms. One poor resident looked at me with those sad, puppy dog eyes and asked if I could help him find a chart before his chief physician arrived. I was willing, but as soon as this nurse saw me, she yelled across the station at me; "What do you think you are doing? He has two eyes and supposedly has graduated from medical school so he can look for his own chart. You need to go back to your business!"

Well that was the end of that. I assume he eventually found the chart, as I never heard screaming, or crying going on during morning rounds. And yes, from time to time you could hear either one of those noises during those long sessions with the residents being drilled for patient information, lab results and diagnostic implications. If they would hesitate or paused, it would be a sure sign of doom. They spent much of their off time researching what they thought might come up during the next rounds so they could survive another day.

One critical detail for rounds with the attending or chief resident was the current lab results. It was the job of the resident to see that the appropriate labs were ordered and the results available for morning. Now these labs have to be drawn by early a.m. in order to be back for rounds. Rounds usually started shortly after 7 a.m., which happens to be around shift change for the nursing staff. One resident forgot to order her labs the day before and came yelling down the hall for a nurse to draw stat labs for her patient. The patient was not in a critical condition and the labs she wanted were routine. When we challenged her, she admitted that she forgot to order them so we should hurry up to get them.

Two things to remember; stat lab work is only for emergencies and yelling never gets you anywhere at shift change unless someone has actually stopped breathing. We explained to her that stat labs were for emergencies, that stat labs cost much more to run and nothing that was not critical was going to happen until shift report was given and the nurses had a chance to get set up for the day. She had to confess to her attending that she blew it but in the end she became much more efficient in ordering her tests.

From pediatrics, baby bottles and little diapers I went to the adult trauma unit, which contained oversized adults, pints of blood and diapers the size of bath towels. This meant the transition from a little poop cleaned with a little baby wipe to an episode of diarrhea that would take three bath towels and a change of clothes, theirs and mine, to clean up. And there is no cuddly smell of baby shampoo in the trauma unit. No, no there is a whole other smell indeed.

I was challenged at every level here and it is here that I learned the most about the value of life and the tragedy of death. It was a great and horrible place at the same time. The staff survived letting off emotional strain with some bizarre, inappropriate and hysterical humor. I can see no other way they could cope. Those who look from the outside do not tend to understand and sometimes consider the staff insensitive when they hear or see some of the activities. But they are faced with life and death every single day which requires great resilience and that is different for each person. Just as in the outside world, each nurse has their coping and defense mechanism.

After a two-year stint, I had reached my emotional peak. I was tired from working nights and working so many of them. Many people recovered but I had seen so much death and suffering I decided that I needed something more positive, proactive and in the daylight. I learned that I am an emotional pasty. I stick immediately to a patient and cannot get loose until they leave, no matter which floor they go to.

A position opened for an ostomy nurse (someone who works with patients who have colostomies, ileostomies, urostomies or wounds). Everyone in the trauma unit had one of these so I was awarded the job because of my years of experience with such things. I quickly became absorbed with my position and the research related to it. I worked under a world-renowned vascular surgeon whose expertise was wound care. He encouraged me in every way and opened many opportunities for me to learn, research, and eventually lecture. It is the career that I am still a part of today and it is very rewarding in that it has allowed me to make recommendations for care while getting to see the results. This physician still motivates me today as is evidenced by the fact that I am still in the thick of the ick so to speak. He is an incredible mentor. I don't care what you do in life, everyone needs a great mentor. My husband would likely have preferred me to emulate Julia Childs or Emeril rather than wound care, but you can't pick what you love, right?

Of course like every nurse I know, I have never had just one job. I have moonlit throughout my working life as a school nurse, painter, child care provider, restaurant chef, teacher, author, educator, consultant, volunteer, legal expert witness, home health nurse, wedding coordinator and more. And of course there is the undocumented position of family, friend and neighborhood nurse consultant, resource slash care provider. My point is, many nurses tend to be type AA personalities, codependent, always wanting to interface with the world and nurture wherever opportunity strikes. The one who loves me most, my husband, tells me I have two speeds, moving and sleep. I tend to see this trait in many medical professionals. We want to make the world better and that requires constant motion. And then we collapse.

What never stops accumulating are the memories of a career that has spanned 41 years. Did I just say forty-one? I have seen every venue of medical service from just about every department and the individuals who are forever a part of my collection of dreams and nightmares continue to be added to the mental file cabinet. In order to understand the nurse that you know, the one in your family, the one who made you smile at the office or the one who made you upset at the hospital, it may be helpful to see life from their side. So here is a tiny glimpse into the everyday life for a nurse.

The tales to follow may be about you but most assuredly they are about all of the other people in the hospital. While you are lying in your hospital bed, waiting anxiously for someone to answer the call light, be certain some nurse is genuinely attempting to help you. You see, six million other people want their attention, are causing them a rainbow of emotions, most of which are not permitted at work. Each work minute is layered on top of what is embroidered into the canvas of their being. In the cacophony of sound they are hearing you. Her or his delay lies in what is happening in the life that never sleeps on the other side of the door.

"The door that nobody else will go in at, seems always to swing open widely for me."

Clara Barton: American Civil War Nurse,

Founder of the American National Red Cross

1821-1912

SPECIAL PEOPLE

I spent five years working with disabled children and adults in two very different environments. One was the children's hospital and school. It was privately funded, beautiful and focused on being a "family" environment. The residents were 3 to 18 years in age and required twenty-four hour a day care. The other was the state hospital that I mentioned earlier. Originally a self-sufficient farm, it was old, not beautiful, and was haunted by memories of abuse that at one time in our country's history were not only legal but also acceptable.

One thing was the same at both places, the genuine character of the residents. No matter what the age, they were always honest and transparent. When you work with typical children you get hugs, giggles and have some fun but as they grow up many kids develop some less desirable teen or adult behavior, even if only for a season. But when you work with individuals who have a childlike perception of life, there is no preconceived idea of who or what you should be. They either love you or they don't.

I LOVE my 'kids'. Every day I looked for a chance to give a hug or be sure they were happy. I was often gifted with trinkets, artwork and other special gifts from my "kids". My very favorite gift came from a sweet resident at the state hospital. He was probably about thirty-five years old and had developmental delays. He had been out for his daily walk with the other residents. I was in preparing their medications for the afternoon. He came running in "Nurse Judy, Nurse Judy, Look!" And he held out his hand, which contained the find. His face was beaming from ear to ear, his eyes fixed on me to see my reaction. "Oh how neat" I said. He replied, "It's for you. I love you!" I took it and wrapped it up special then place it in my pocket to take home. He was so excited with his great find that I could not tell him "No Thank You" or reject it even if it was a very dead and decayed frog. And it was! You learn to smile much and wash often in this job. Essential skills for everyday nursing.

"Go into medicine for the right reason. Don't make it about the money---make it about caring for those who need your healing hands. If it isn't in your heart, patients will feel it."

- Palma Iacovitti, Nurse

CAROL

One of my most memorable residents at the state hospital was an eighty three year old lady with syphilis dementia. Her story was so compelling and unfortunately typical of those around in the nineteen teens and twenties. She was a daddy's girl. When her father passed away he left her mother to fend for herself, Carol and her siblings. Her mother had never worked and could not get a decent job, so she sent her daughter out to prostitute for money. By the time she was twenty she had contracted the syphilis and by twenty five had such severe brain damage from it that she was sent to the state hospital where she lived out her days.

Now she remained in amazingly good condition, minus one eye that was removed for a tumor type growth back in the fifties. She could sit with her leg straight up in the air and occasional would speak obscenities I am certain she learned in her youth, none I will repeat and many I can't even spell. I grew up Baptist after all! Most of the time, however, she was quite childlike. She called those she liked "momma" and those she didn't like names in that list I referred to earlier. She liked me and would often come looking for "momma".

It would be during the early eighties the government began doing studies on whether or not hormone replacement therapy versus menstruation protected your bones better. This government funded study was conducted at the state hospital. This gal had not had her "time" for thirty years or so. They decided to try a hormone regimen that would stimulate the female cycle and hopefully improve bone density. Carol was selected due to her age.

One day she started screaming from her infirmary room "Momma, Momma, come quick." I raced in and there she was on the toilet. She pulled my face close to her one good eye shouting, "Look, Look!" and sobbing uncontrollably. She had started her period and she was devastated. I had to try to explain "Why" to a woman who couldn't understand why she was suddenly having her "time" again. I can't even explain why I am still having my time some days, so imagine how you would explain it to someone with the understanding of a three or four year old. I spent quite a bit of time with her, hugged her and finally settled with suggesting, "Let's wait a couple days and see if it goes away." She was happy with that and of course it did go away, for that month. Fortunately they only did this to her, and us, for about five months. She was delighted, to say the least, when it never returned.

"It is not how much you do, but how much love you put in the doing."

- Mother Theresa

Deborah

Deborah was mentally delayed and had a severe pica appetite (eats any and every thing, not necessarily in the edible category). When she was first brought in to the state hospital in the sixties an emergency surgery was performed and they found more than seventy objects including paperclips, ink pens, large laundry bag safety pins, bottle caps, nails, staples, glass and dozens of other items. Amazingly she had no intestinal damage. The next thirty or so years would be spent trying to prevent her from eating inappropriate objects. In the early years they would resort to using electrical charges similar to a dog collar, shock therapy, ice therapy, numerous medications and straight jacket type restraints. They ended nearly twenty years later with the best result being a zipped up suit and a helmet. This would keep her from hiding things for snacking on later or from eating inappropriate objects. The entire area had to be secured knowing the smallest particle would become a garnish to her dinner. A twenty-four hour a day effort. In the thirty or so years she never lost her appetite for the inedible.

Nurses are patient people. *~Author Unknown*

Robert

Robert suffered from autism. He was about thirty-five, dark haired and very handsome. In a crowd or picture you would not be able to pick him out. He always had to have his clothes neat and perfect, his dishes all absolutely straight and the rooms clean in order to be content. Most people did not pay much attention to him. I would go into his unit at the state hospital and as I would be standing at the medication cupboard he would walk up and stand silently right behind me. After I was done passing evening medications, I would go sit down on the sofa in the dayroom and wait. Eventually he would come and sit by me. He would rock and talk or sing. If you did not pay attention you might think it was gibberish. But if you listened, he would be repeating whatever was on television or commenting on it. He was quite detailed in his observations.

One night they were talking about how many days until Christmas. He sat down next to me and repeated the Christmas news. I said, "I like Christmas songs." And he started singing Christmas songs, and he sang several. I just sat and listened. He would lean on my arm and sing and smile. Inside that mysterious mind was someone very aware of his environment but unable to figure out a way to get free of his box. But every once in a while, you would make contact and it was awesome. It made it worthwhile for me to let him know I knew he was there, and every once in a while he would let me know he was too.

Arthur and Ted

In the thirties two brothers were brought to the state hospital at the ages of eight and ten. Their mother had passed away and the father did not want to raise them so he brought them to the facility. He never came back. These two boys were perfectly normal when they arrived, but this was in the days where those unthinkable things were happening in the state institutions. When they would have an accident in their pants, they would be stripped down naked and placed in a cement room and hosed down with a high power hose, then left to dry sometime for hours. They might even get their meal in there. The thought of that is unspeakable.

Over time, due to lack of education and nurturing, and likely as a result of the environment, they regressed. The older brother Ted, maintained most of his social abilities however he never gained ground intellectually. The younger brother Arthur quit speaking about six months after he arrived and he never spoke again. He was constantly anxious, and always had a worried look on his face. He paced a lot and sat in a fetal position (all curled up) wringing his hands. He would come up to you, look at you with those sad brown eyes and at the most whimper.

Sometimes he would let you hold his hand then he would run back to his chair. I felt so sad for these boys. They were still just young boys.

It was the younger brother that had severe asthma. He would end up in the infirmary and need epinephrine and breathing treatments. I would have my first scare with giving the wrong dose of a medication. I was so pleased that he had improved during the night though he never slept, just sat in the chair calmly all night. Found out that there is a great deal of importance in a decimal point in giving the right dose. The doctor had not included a leading '0' and I did not see a dot on the line so I gave the wrong dose. WOW, I cannot tell you how glad I am for a good outcome. Lesson learned; Always ask for a zero and a decimal then look it up to be sure!

The Button

One resident left me with a lifetime souvenir,

a twisted muscle in my arm. This gentleman was mentally challenged and also suffered from psychological problems as well. He was tall, lean and extremely powerful when provoked. He was obsessed with buttons. He didn't care what they looked like, how big they were or whose shirt he took them off of. If he was going to stay calm he had to have a button. This was general knowledge to those working at the facility. We went to great measures to be sure he had his button as he became extremely violent if it was lost.

A new employee was trying to get this gentleman to follow a direction, which he refused to do. So the new employee decided that he was going to try to coerce him by taking away the button. I was standing at the medication cupboard at the time with my back to the room. All of the sudden I had a set of teeth locked firmly on my left arm and twisting the muscle underneath.

I knew immediately who it had to be and what incited this attack. "Where is his button?" I yelled, to which the newbie replied "I took it away"! One of the other staff heard the commotion and came running in. "Give it back now!" Problem was the new employee couldn't find it, anywhere. Finally the veteran staff ran over and ripped a button off the new guy's jacket and gave it to the distressed resident who immediately released my arm. He did not break the skin but there was a huge raised mass with deep teeth marks. And the muscle remains raised and twisted today. I have never forgotten that resident, or the new employee for that fact. I think it was possibly his last day in that unit. And it may also explain my fascination with buttons, I have them everywhere.

MARY

"She is missing, has anybody seen her?" A panicked room mother was searching the building for dear little Mary. Mary was a rambunctious girl that gave new meaning to the word "fast." She could leave your sight in a split second and be half way across the street in less than sixty seconds. This was well known, as one day while turning our heads to acknowledge our boss, she disappeared, split and run. The property was searched everywhere and I do mean every nook and cranny inside and out. If she wasn't found calls would need to be made to the family. The police had already been called. They didn't need a picture; they had done this search before.

It would be twenty minutes or so when a call was received from a neighbor to the school. The neighbor had been working in her backyard. When she came in the house she heard her toilet flushing, and flushing. She was terrified and called the police then picked up her broom and walked down the hall to see who was there. She was shocked to see the intruder, a little girl standing on her toes, flushing the toilet over and over and laughing at each "splurge". This was the greatest fun this little girl had had for a while. Who knew this would be the entertainment that could hold her attention for more than sixty consecutive seconds giving the school the time needed to recover her.

Wendy

Wendy was a beautiful little girl, who had cerebral palsy, needing full assistance to eat. She was bright with a great sense of humor. She would laugh easily at things, such as noise. Problem was when she laughed she would tense up and clamp her mouth shut, grinding her teeth. This would not have been a huge problem if, on this one particular occasion, my finger had not been in her mouth. "Never put your fingers in her mouth!" I knew this, but I had given her a bite and it was stuck to the side of her mouth. I reached in to move it and a loud noise startled her. She jumped then started laughing. I was stuck, and in terrible pain. The entire room had cracked up from the noise so I had to first get everyone else to calm down, and then hope she would too. She did eventually let go of my finger, and as you can see, it works today. But I have never put my finger in someone else's mouth again, not even my own!

Leslie

Born to an underage mother with a drinking problem and a father who had his own addictive problems, Leslie found her way to the crippled children's' school at an early age. She was diagnosed very early with Fetal Alcohol Syndrome. She was projected to do poorly with life skills, cognitive learning and behavioral adaptation. Her parents could not handle her by the age of three so she was placed full time at the school. She had some real challenging behavior at times requiring constant supervision. At other times she was a true delight, a sweet little girl.

The school closed three times a year, spring, early fall and over the winter holidays. The children either had to go to their homes or to a foster care home for these mandatory breaks. It was after one of those breaks that the horror of sexual abuse directed toward a child became a reality for one of the girls. During a playtime I observed her doing some inappropriate things with dolls, things a child who has fetal alcohol syndrome and is mentally delayed would not know. I contacted the social worker and through a careful psychological and medical evaluation it was determined that she had been molested.

I was devastated to think that a parent could do that. Innocence lost at the hands of those who are supposed to love and protect you, this was completely out of my mental file drawer. And to further my disillusionment was the directive of the protective services to continue to permit home visits. While I would like to say this was the only time I saw this I cannot. As a matter of fact the number of abuse cases at the county hospital contributed immensely to my moving on to other healthcare areas. And the abuse does not stop with children I am afraid to say. Nurses see this on a daily basis, children, parents, grandparents, and strangers. Horrible crimes committed against vulnerable people.

"Most of the important things in the world have been accomplished by people who have kept on trying when there seemed to be no hope at all."

– Dale Carnegie, American writer

VICTORIA

One young gal started coming to the day program at the children's school when she was about five. Her elderly foster parents would bring her in and it was evident that they cared for her. But she would cry and cry with a high pitched noise for hours on end sometimes. I tried a number of things to calm her down without success. It was a tragedy of the greatest proportions. She had been abused as an infant. Her father had thrown her against the wall because she would not stop crying. When that did not work he hit her head against a table several times until there was no more noise. He put her in the crib. When her mother came home and found her she realized something had happened and brought her to the hospital. She would be nearly blind, only seeing glimpses of light or images, seizure prone, unable to walk, and be mentally retarded all because of the anger of her father.

It was one day while combing her hair in the bathroom that she stopped crying. I had turned her chair so that she was facing the mirror and as I ran the comb through her hair she started smiling. So I talked to her, combed her hair and washed her face. She made a noise that equated to a laugh for her and then it happened she smiled. So this became our routine for her and it was sheer joy to know that for moment, she was happy. And she had the most beautiful smile. It was the highlight of my day to see something as wonderful as this pure joy expressed her smiles and laughter. www.childhelp.org

BABY FIX

I worked for years with children in a variety of settings. It is a wonderful and devastating profession, this nursing. Children come into the medical system for a number of reasons from illness to abuse.

It is nearly impossible not to fall in love with every child under the age of two the very minute they get there. And when their parents leave and the crying stops they cling to the nurse like their life depends on it. Some parents bring their children to the hospital, leave and never come back until the doctor says they need to go home or to child protective services. Sometimes they may be in for several weeks. In many cases the diagnoses for these beautiful babies would rock you to the core.

Sara

One of the children that stayed with me the longest was a little two-month old baby girl. She had arrived to the hospital for a possible broken arm from falling off the bed. Since two month olds don't roll over the story did not quite hold up. It was downright stinky. They admitted her and did a series of x-rays only to find numerous broken bones of various ages. Child Protective Services was quickly notified and the parents were forbidden to visit until a full investigation could be done.

I immediately fell in love with this beautiful little girl and could not imagine what type of mind it would take to break the bones of a baby. I thought about all the pain she had experienced in her short life and wondered if she had ever been without it. I could not put her down the nights I worked. I would do all my work, get the rest of the babies to sleep and then hold her, rocking for long periods of time. She would snuggle up to me and seemed to relax. I could have stayed there day and night if they would have let me.

Her bones slowly mended. To our complete dismay the court decided to give her to the fathers parents who lived in town. These people had been around this girl and never reported the bruising. The medical team did not agree with this at all and tried everything to persuade the court to no avail. Just about the time for discharge they determined a need to do some more testing which fortunately also provided a little more time to work with the justice system. The court moved instead to award custody to the mothers' parents who lived out of state. The parents had already stated they would go wherever she was sent and continue to try to get her back. It was also discovered that the maternal grandfather had abused the mother when she was young.

The court stayed with the decision and ordered her release. I always wonder what happened to this precious baby. It still puzzles me that in the protective service divisions that they are more concerned about meeting the goal of reuniting children with "family" even though there is strong indication that the abuse goes deep in the clan. It is statistically rare to find immediate rehabilitation for violence in a short anger management course especially if there is not a period of time set for observation. And for an infant who cannot defend itself, well, the thought is grave. The day she left and we had to give her to the authorities was one of my worst. As I looked around the floor I was not alone in my extreme sadness.

Joe

As the physician entered the room he saw a cute one week old boy. All the cooing and squirming inside the blue baby blank could not be mistaken. This adorable little boy was about to get circumcised. The treatment room was set up for the procedure. The baby was placed in the little papoose board and wrapped up like a sweet little Christmas present. Once secured, he was unwrapped so that only his "equipment" was showing. The nurse scrubbed the area and called the doctor in. Of course all that cold wet scrub caused the baby to become a bit upset.

Well the physician entered with confidence. With his sterile gown on, gloves and mask in place he slowly picked up the scalpel, pulled back the blanket and immediately received a ceremonial baptism. Straight shot to the face, that's right, warm, yellow and a perfect stream. A string of words that I don't use and that babies shouldn't hear came flowing out of his mouth while the urine was dripping from his glasses. Ugh. So he threw down the blanket, pulled off his gear and raced to the bathroom to remove the offensive liquid. After several minutes and with a little more reservation he returned to the task at hand only this time he leaned back while pulling the blanket back just to make sure the fountain was off. A successful circumcision was performed and everyone left happy, well, you know what I mean.

Caring is the essence of nursing.

~Jean Watson

The Code Man

RSV is a respiratory virus that in adults acts like a cold but in babies it causes severe respiratory problems. For a long period of time the treatment of choice was a drug administered through tubing that ran into a hood sitting over the babies' head. At the county hospital it was not unusual to have six such babies in one room. The fog from the mist was so thick that you almost couldn't see the nurse running in circles in the middle of the room. It would be a few years later they would decide that the treatment was not that effective and that the fog in which we spent twelve hours a shift in was indeed harmful to the nurse but not the virus. Oh joy.

RSV would make breathing a real effort for the little ones and they would become tired and fussy from all the work. The swing was often the only thing that would provide them some relief, as they would be able to sit up making it a bit easier to get a breath. And then there was the snot, lots of it. It was an endless battle to keep their noses clear which was critical as babies are obligate nose breathers (breath only through their noses) until about six months. If you can imagine your worst cold and then picture yourself with six noses then you have a good idea what I am referring to.

It was an intern (not a full doctor yet) who provided unnecessary rescuing for one particular infant. He came into the room to assess his patient who was breathing quite rapidly and was wheezing. Key word here is "breathing". I don't know what picture or thought passed through his mind, if any, but he suddenly picked up the baby and ran toward the Intensive Care Unit shouting "Code Blue" which would imply someone was not "breathing". This tiny alarmed baby was screaming all the way down the hall. Hmmmm. Immediately we would wonder just exactly where he placed the stethoscope listening only to determine there was a potential problem.

We were fairly certain if we did not calm the

intern down he would be the next to code. Once we got him under control he admitted that perhaps the baby had not stopped breathing "completely" and he was sure that as he was aspiring to be pediatrician he would be able to correctly identify that body function in the future. We offered to return the now once again quiet, "breathing" baby to his swing and suggested the physician try finding a quiet corner to swing or sleep in as well.

"Healing the spirit is as important as healing the body." *Sally Karioth (Zadra, 2005)*

Angel

Long term patients were always tough as you become surrogate parents in a way, at their side day and night. We were privileged to have a long-term relationship with a little girl who was born with several congenital problems. She was dependent on the ventilator to keep her breathing and a feeding tube to provide her nutrition. She was adorable and had personality plus. She had a fantastic family who so desperately wanted her home. We were her extended family and we spoiled her rotten. What was great about her were these big, round, chubby cheeks and a smile that went ear to ear, and we would get her to laugh so hard her eyes would tear. Watching her laugh was almost as fun because she made no noise due to the trach (tube in the neck for breathing) but her whole body shook. We decorated her space for every holiday and had a huge celebration for her first birthday.

It was not long after that the physicians had determined that her time would be short and if the family ever wanted to have her home this would be the way she would have to go. The family decided to take her home and they got to enjoy almost three months with her. She passed away in her sleep. The hardest and most touching funeral I had ever gone to was hers. There were pictures of her lining the funeral home and a video running that the family had captured at home. It was good to see her have the same fun at home that we watched her have in the hospital. And when she was buried, we each let a balloon go as a symbol of the journey she had just taken. It was a beautiful sight to see tons of red balloons floating toward the sky with the sun shining bright behind us. It was one of few times we were able to experience closure for the loss of one of "our kids."

During this same period of time there was another baby girl with a heart defect who was in the next bed. Her parents were illegal immigrants thus she was not an American citizen. Why this mattered from the medical perspective is that the only chance she had for survival was to have a heart transplant. Unfortunately the organ donor foundation would not put her on the list to receive one because of her lack of citizenship. We essentially had one option, watch her slowly die. And we did. She was also a sweet baby, lots of smiles and hugs, and a precious family. We celebrated her first birthday too and she passed away not long after. The passion of nursing is healing and it was so difficult to know that there might be a solution and we had no hope of accessing it. Two beds, two beautiful girls, two totally difficult situations. Our role was to care for them the same, giving them what science and agencies could not.

"When you're a nurse you know that every day you will touch a life or a life will touch yours."

~ Author Unknown

Mindy

When you look at children you think about sweet smelling and cuddly things, usually. One particular night a young patient suffered what appeared to be appendicitis. After some testing they discovered that the appendix actually ruptured and had to be removed emergently. As is typical a cap was placed on her head before taking her into the operating room. After all you would not want hair in a surgical wound, right? Well the patient arrived to the floor after her surgery. No complications were reported so we began by doing the initial assessment and getting the patient comfortable. We removed the hat and all this dirt literally "jumped" onto the pillowcase. A wee bit closer look would reveal that this "dirt" was still moving! As it turned out what we were looking at was lice, tons of them. We discovered that these wingless insects that live on hair and feed on skin are apparently not fond of anesthesia and they were making great strides to abandon ship.

When we realized this uninvited company was in the room with the patient we quickly changed all the linen and got an order for a shampoo designed to get rid of icky lice. We spent the rest of the night itching, not that anything was there, but the thought of something being there was enough to drive us crazy. I can honestly say for the next few days we resembled monkeys picking through each other's hair looking for nits (lice eggs). We had a party to celebrate a nit free experience. When you work at night you have a party to celebrate just about anything you could imagine. I think I am getting itchy.......

Sex Education?

The twelve year old was admitted for what the

mother thought was appendicitis. She was certain that the pains her daughter was having had to be that. During the admission history and physical it was discovered that the young lady had been having her "monthly time" for about a year. The girl then revealed that she had not had her "monthly time" for a few (seven) months and was having cramping. Upon careful examination it was discovered that, you guessed it, she was pregnant. Twelve years old! A long discussion was had with the mother who initially sat quietly, then, after deep thought revealed that "it must have happened when a young man had punched her in the stomach." She was dead serious. An indepth anatomy lesson would be necessary. After hearing all the details associated with becoming pregnant the mother stated "she can't be pregnant because she couldn't have had sex, she is only twelve." We assured her that she indeed could have sex at twelve and at some point she had!

Here it was in living color, children having children. A subject you see on television but never think you will see it in real life. The sad part is that like this mother, many parents don't think their young children have or can have sex for one reason or another. Consider this your public service announcement: Parents, kids can and do have sex. And as a grandma, you will be raising your child AND your grandchild! I would be thinking about having a talk soon, even if you are sure you don't need to. Oh, and to be clear, they can have sex even if they live at home, make good grades, don't date or have never seen The Graduate.

Beautiful

Babies are supposed to arrive perfect, ten toes and ten fingers. Most do, but some do not. It does not make them less human, just different. In one way or another we are all different. When parents have planned a certain life for themselves these "abnormalities" cause quite a crisis for them. Thousands of babies are put aside to starve or up for adoption in many countries just because they are girls or disabled and the family can only keep one baby. Shocking, but in the hospital we see that happen right here in our country. It is hidden under some other pretense, but it happens every day. Parents so concerned with their image or idea of 'the perfect life' that they will cast aside children born with "defects." I am not speaking of those who wisely decide they would not be able to parent a child, such as a young teenager or a drug addict. I am speaking of those who are too embarrassed, ashamed or self-involved to step up.

A beautiful baby was born, blond hair, ten fingers, ten toes and Down syndrome. The mom had an emergency cesarean section so she was not able to see the baby right away. The father was so upset by the diagnosis of Down syndrome that he insisted both he and the mom sign over their parental rights and put her up for adoption. He refused to let the mother see her little girl. No need to hold her or get attached, it would be unacceptable. I wonder what these families would do if the spouse or their other typical child became disabled, would they cast them aside too? Ah, but I digress. Down syndrome is not unfamiliar to society and these children live happy typical lives and often now are able to achieve quite a lot in our world thanks to therapy and early intervention. Some even able to go to college, hold jobs, marry and live completely independent lives.

Should that family actually have gone through with adopting out their baby they would have missed hugs, kisses, tears, laughter, smiles and utter devotion. Fortunately they did not. This mom, when she was able to see her daughter, fell in love. The husbands' employer challenged that dad to face his fears and step up to his responsibilities. Mom and dad ended up taking their baby home and within a week the mother was determined that if dad couldn't handle it, he could leave because her daughter wasn't going anywhere. Dad didn't leave, and that family was forever changed. I am certain they will forever change the lives of others as well.

Adorable

Another young baby girl arrived on schedule in the labor and delivery department. She was adorable, nurses fighting to hold her and each one trying to name her. Nurses in the neonatal intensive care units are passionate and protective of their charges. With a planned adoption, the arrival of this child should have been occasion for celebration for both the birth mom and the adoptive family. It appeared an unexpected situation was present. The adoptive family decided they didn't want to go through with it if she wasn't normal. They hung up and withdrew paperwork. The birth mom, who had already made wise plans to provide a home for her child now, was faced with a dilemma. Now what?

A call was placed to a nurse and parent who already had a Down syndrome child to see if they had interest or ideas. The mother desperately wanted to bring this treasure home, but it was not the right time for the family. But she did have some ideas. Through a series of phone calls and emails, a family was found who had been waiting to adopt a special needs child.

The agencies were able to coordinate the adoption on the very day she would have been discharged to CPS (Child Protective Services) which is often one long life of multiple foster care home transitions. As a matter of fact a recent report in our state reported over 10,000 children in the foster care system with less than 50% finishing school and moving from home to home an average of three times a year.

It was instant affirmation when baby met family. The family shared that one of their other children had actually prayed exactly nine months prior for a new baby. She even looked like her adoptive family. Nurses do not often get to partake in making a life altering event like this occur. It was wonderful for them to see their little charge, dressed in pink, be carried out with a family full of excitement. Awesome! www.sharingds.org www.reecesrainbow.org

"I have an almost complete disregard of precedent, and a faith in the possibility of something better. It irritates me to be told how things have always been done. I defy the tyranny of precedent. I go for anything new that might improve the past."

Clara Barton: American Civil War Nurse,

Founder of the American National Red Cross,

1821-1912

TEACHING THE MASSES

Nursing extends beyond the walls of nursing homes, hospitals, private homes and clinics to the very community in which we live and all around the globe. Nurses volunteer hundreds of hours every year. Despite long and often emotional days providing care to those who are ill they step into yet another nursing role to administer immunizations at the grocery store, check blood pressures in their churches, teach dietary practices for diabetics in senior citizen centers and plan or participate in community fund raising events that raise awareness about health care issues such as the Down Syndrome Buddy Walk or the Susan G. Komen Breast Cancer Walk. Nurses are everywhere and many of them look forward to those opportunities to arm the public with a little more information giving them tools for better health and improve the general quality of life.

In one community an annual CPR event was held. It was for the lay (non-medical) community. Thousands of teens and adults would go through stations to learn how to do CPR and to save choking babies, children and adults. CPR is a tremendous skill that requires only your hands to possibly save the life of another human being. It is always a rewarding experience to see people learn this simple skill and to see them feel empowered as they go back to their homes, families and work. Oh, by the way, it works!

In addition nurses may be found checking cholesterol or blood sugar or giving classes on the signs and symptoms of colon cancer. While one would think such presentations with graphic details and pictures would be unappealing to the elderly, it is quite the opposite. Seems as people age they become more interested in discussing those subjects in great detail. They often ask so many vivid questions and request such graphic detail that nurses learn to never shy away from giving the complete, unrated, full color version on any topic.

Nurses also travel around the globe to serve and share their gifts. In third world countries classes are taught on health and hygiene to college students. While those in some countries bathe in the same rivers in which they bury their dead and void in, discussion on clean water and regular hygiene are essential. The nurse is challenged with being prepared to problem solve issues such as a two or three mile walk to a clean water well, the cost of soap being prohibitive for people who earn only dollars a month or the lack of fire materials to even boil water. The greatest challenge for me was having age appropriate material for the college students I was charged to teach while in India. They were all around the ripe age of fourteen. Fourteen year olds are not focused on their adult health and hygiene needs even in third world countries. Their concerns are typical for their age, purely hormonal, but the opportunity exists to answer all their questions and still deliver some information they may use later on in life. A nurse must always be prepared, much like the girl scouts who provided me that foundational truth.

Nurses are drawn like magnets to get on the first plane to join rescue teams or to provide services in disaster areas, such as the floods in Louisiana or the hurricane in Haiti. Donations of supplies are solicited and with great pride are donated in enormous quantities for nurses to carry to each of these relief areas. The work in these situations is some of the toughest a nurse will face. They are forever changed by what they see and are asked to do.

Choosing who will be rescued from a rooftop as you triage from your boat, who will get medication when doses are limited, who will be provided food or water. It is a humbling setting for anyone. A nurse is faced not only with the limitation of resources in these dire situations but with the inevitable and fragile state of life, an element that is completely out of their control.

One of my favorite experiences is as a teacher. Teaching nursing and medical students, you see their eyes wide open and their faces grimace at the stories and pictures they see. They cannot imagine that they will be able to see or handle the numerous situations that are covered in class. The first year or so they are green, easily grossed out by the day-to-day stuff the old timers call a job. But the truth is once they have graduated, passed their licensure exam and have a good year under their belts, they will be able to eat dinner while discussing blood and bowel movements without the least bit of nausea. Those shows on television with the graphic details won't even faze them. It is most likely that any good nurse or doctor will tell you what's wrong whether you are interested or not.

And of course once family and friends know a nurse is licensed, whether as a nursing assistant or a registered nurse, you are on twenty-four hour call to the entire world. Really! Do we mind? No. I have yet to meet a peer that is offended that we are considered knowledgeable and able to help our clan decide what care they need and where to get it. This includes an urgent summons to help an anxious new mother determine if she has exposed her child to a communicable disease by trying a shirt on her baby in the department store, a request to check a mother's blood pressure, or to see if symptoms a father was having were a sign of a heart attack. Strangers at the grocery store will see a uniform or badge and ask questions about their rash and whether or not certain foods can be eaten since they have diabetes. It is a non-stop job.

Most will tell you that as a nurse they are their own worst enemy when it comes to their health.

Many will diagnose and treat themselves and each other before they will consult with their physician. "Nurse heal thyself" is a common practice, as we don't want to be a burden or take time away from those who need us. And the truth is we will have to tell the doctor what's wrong anyway, right? Every nurse I know has come to work under less than optimal circumstances. An illness, crisis at home, overtime, and the list goes on. Perhaps it is the "nurture" nature that is part of the nursing character. We simply are driven to care more for others than ourselves. It is no small wonder that at times your nurse may seem tired or distracted. They are taking care of the world! And now back to the 80's.

"I am only one; but still I am one. I cannot do everything; but still I can do something. And because I cannot do everything, I will not refuse to do the something that I can do." *– E.E. Hale,*

LIFE IN THE FAST LANE

Working on an ambulance allows you to meet people in their most undignified, vulnerable and devastating situations. Every day is an adventure as it is impossible to predict providential events. Each day brings high adrenaline rushes and hours of waiting. It is a sad irony that in order to stay employed in the health profession others must experience some event. Not every call on the ambulance is tragic. Sometimes people call for trivial problems, truthfully, loneliness or holiday blues would be the official diagnosis. But that isn't covered by insurance, so it might be shortness of breath or maybe a little chest pain that is reported.

Moe

One gentleman called for chest pain that would not resolve with nitroglycerin tablets. He was a young man who had interestingly enough never been diagnosed with any heart disease. We got to his house, and naturally, he was in the basement. One hundred year old Midwest homes are constructed with stairs steep enough to make nice people say bad words. Imagine if you will a flight of fifteen stairs with a pitch of, say, 160 degrees. The staircase is all of two and a half feet wide and the young patient states he can't walk "up" them. You guessed it, a stretcher in the chair position, being hoisted up by two very tall individuals. My back has never been the same. We finally got him to the ambulance where we began our assessment. He had a normal blood pressure, pulse, temperature, respiratory rate and a headache, likely from all the nitro he had taken. Of course we are not sure why he had nitro in the first place, but that will be for the physician to discuss.

I was trying my best to be sensitive to his

pain, though in all honesty this was likely a case of anxiety related to some marital discord. He *requested* some oxygen to help him breathe better. In removing the tubing from the connection on the portable canister, the tubing stuck. I had to use full force to pull it off the portable tank. It suddenly came apart and the speed of my hand was uncontrollable and I slugged him right square in the forehead. "Oh, are you trying to kill me?" I felt horrible and apologized profusely. He forgave me and was none the worse for wear. And I managed to get his oxygen on. By the time we reached the hospital he was sitting up talking and ready to go home. The trip was thirteen miles long.

KEITH

An ambulance call came in late one night about two in the morning. Everyone drove to the station and jumped into the ambulance. The call was to a house where the roommate came home and couldn't wake up his buddy. The men were elderly widowers sharing a basement apartment. When we arrived, the gentleman was in the kitchen with the police officer that was trying to keep him distracted. We took one look Keith and knew this roommate was not going to wake up anytime soon. He was cool to the touch and a little blue. He had apparently decided to stay home from his weekly card game at the VFW and had died in the chair while watching television. We informed his roommate who became even more distraught. They were both in their eighties and had lived together for a long time. It was heartbreaking and we were all a bit teary.

What happened next was a bit more challenging. When we went to put his body on the stretcher we could not straighten it out. He had evidently been deceased in the chair for quite some time, hours, and his body maintained the sitting position. We had to keep the roommate distracted while we got the body to the ambulance. I am completely unaware as to how the mortuary straightened him out, but since the casket was straight I am certain they figured it out.

"To do what nobody else will do, a way that nobody else can do,

in spite of all we go through; is to be a nurse."

- Rawsi Williams

Peter

People driving in the country tend to do so very fast. Wide open spaces. There are no police radars and you can definitely see the cop car coming from miles away. Add gravel roads to the mix with a little alcohol and you've got disaster written all over it. It was dinnertime and the pager went off. It was a stat call so I raced to the station and we were on our way. What we knew initially was there was a rollover accident with someone ejected into a field. As we approached the car it did not look promising. It appeared that the car had rolled several times. And we could not see the driver, anywhere.

When we stopped we were flagged over to the middle of a cornfield. The young man was groaning, pale and in shock. We applied life pants; a giant set of pants that function like a blood pressure cuff to help keep the blood pressure up. We started an I.V. and sped to the local hospital to get some meds on board. The local hospital had no trauma capabilities so the patient was to going to be transferred and we set out for the hospital up the road, a mere 31 miles. This was a record setting trip and it seemed like eternity while we were going. The plus was that the roads were straight and empty. The down side was that his blood pressure was low, his pulse was weak, and he would stop breathing every couple of minutes. I "talked" to him the entire way. I quickly discovered that if I tapped his cheek firmly he would gasp and we would get another minute or two. I reassured him no one had died in my ambulance and he was not going to change that.

We called ahead to the emergency room and told them what we suspected for injures and reported his blood alcohol was .325 at the community hospital. That alone should have killed him. They must have sensed the anxiety in my calls and believed my assessment as they had a surgeon ready and the staff immediately rolled him straight to the operating room. We waited for him to come out as we were required to wait to collect our life pants, as those are a pricey item. We were told they were able to repair him, though he would be critical for some time. His blood alcohol peaked at .40, a level at which all people lose consciousness and some die thus they used very little anesthesia. It would be six weeks before he would have a 0 blood alcohol level. As he recovered he was able to tell people my name and every word I said on the ride to the hospital. You just never know what the last word heard will be so speak well always as someone will remember it.

He did recover completely and after twelve weeks returned to the military base back east. They required him to go through a twelve-step program to deal with the drinking problems. He lost his drivers' license for one year, which I think is pretty light for the extensive damage he caused to himself and could have caused to others.

Grandpa Willy

Okay, at this point I must say, beware of senior citizen centers serving chicken. I must follow this with a caution about the events that occurred at this senior citizen center. Because many elderly folks have poor teeth, bridges, crowns or dentures, they often tend to chew poorly, the large pieces of barely touched food can effectively plug the airway while going down, and I can tell you it can smell very bad on the way back up. On this particular day a frantic call was placed from the senior center to the ambulance service. Grandpa had suddenly fallen to the floor while setting up for checkers and he was looking quite bad.

We arrived to find a collection of elderly folk trying everything to revive their companion from slapping his cheeks to pushing on his stomach. Once the sea of people were parted better assessment could be made to confirm what we already knew, he had indeed stopped breathing. And, as expected, he had no pulse. As we attempted to begin CPR, those around shouted recommendations from "give him water" and "sit him up". Several kept suggesting we just "give him oxygen" clearly not aware of the intent of performing CPR.

As I began to give him the first two breaths, a first for my nursing career, he vomited his lunch. I would like to say it didn't touch me but this was long before mouth shields unfortunately. We turned him over and cleaned his mouth, then started again. We administered CPR for quite some time (27 minutes to be exact) when we had to admit there was no response. We were on the communication box a.k.a. CB with the physician during the event and after the appropriate time was reached, we declared he had indeed expired.

We drove him to the coroner and then we returned to the station. It was the first time I had done CPR, and it is a vivid memory still with me today. We learn CPR and are told we can save lives. And we often can. But it is a frustrating thing to know that even with the skills and medications and technology, you cannot always succeed. It is back to that undeniable truth that at some point, we are all destined for the same end. I cried for some time, and spent an inordinate amount of time washing out my mouth. Suddenly as if by design we were sent out on another emergency call. Mourning was over.

"By medicine life may be prolonged, yet death will seize the doctor too"

William Shakespeare

Jim Beam

Medical people can be summoned to any location on the planet. This particular day the local pub called. They reported that a customer had fallen off the stool and was unresponsive. You may now be using untapped medical skills if you are imagining why a man in a bar would fall off a stool. This would be called critical thinking! We brought the stretcher into the dark, crowded smoke-filled bar to collect our patient. We suspected it was more likely that he passed out as opposed to suffering from a medical event. An assessment was initiated and we were not able to arouse him with the usual methods recommended to evoke a response. Don't ask.

Our suspicions were confirmed in dramatic fashion as we went to load the stretcher into the ambulance. The dear soul came to, and in a flurry of movement attempted to punch my lights out.

Fortunately I was able to miss the blow or I would have been the next one on the stretcher. We kindly restrained our charge for the ride to the hospital. Many verbal insults were tossed around during the ride to the hospital but I believe once he sobered up he went home without injury. Whether he has any memory of the night is a whole other matter entirely. I, on the other hand, have continued to keep my "weave and bob" skills honed.

RICHIE

An emergency call took the ambulance to the state hospital which housed mentally challenged children and adults. A sweet resident, about thirty, was outside on the playground. He fell off the swing and hit his head. He did not get up. We took him to the hospital up the road, which means the next town, as they had the ability to do neurological exams such as CT (cat scans) and EEG's. When he was taken into the emergency room one of the staff looked at him and remarked "Oh it's just a state hospital guy". My dander was up. "What do you mean by that?" She replied "Well, he's just a retarded guy from the school!"

"He is a human being and he is injured. He is capable of laughing, playing and giving a hug to those around him. He deserves your care just as much as the next guy. I don't think you have a clue what …….."! My partner quickly dragged me aside and the physician asked the nurse to leave. I was appalled that a person's residence or ability might affect the care they may receive. He did get good treatment and returned to the state hospital, his home. That great care may well be the result of my tirade in the emergency room. I learned not all people see all life as having equal value. I have never used the word retard, even when it was an approved term used to refer to those who are developmentally delayed. I never will. www.r-word.org

> **"I realize that patriotism is not enough.**
>
> **I must have no hatred or bitterness towards**
>
> **anyone."**
>
> *Edith Cavell*

ARE YOU OKAY???

Never assume people lying on the street are dead or even in distress. An ambulance call took us downtown to main street (it was the only street) where a man had been laying for several hours without moving. It was interesting in that first, he lay there several hours before we were called and secondly no one had try to rustle him awake. Hmmm. Anyway the consensus on the street was that people thought maybe he was sick or had died so they called.

I grabbed my stethoscope and ran to his aid. He did not need it. At the very moment I bent over his eyes opened. He screamed, I screamed and this medical assessment was complete. I eventually got my heart rate down. After talking to the freshly revived and now fed street sleeper I suggested he try a park bench or a home for sleeping next time. Perhaps just a well-placed sign might avoid another nightmare on main street.

"Our job as nurses is to cushion the sorrow and celebrate the joy,

Every day, while we are 'just doing our jobs.'"

- Christine Belle, RN, BSN

URGENT (EMERGENT) CARE

The urgent care and emergency room waiting areas are always crazy. It seems that everyone gets sick at the same time, that or the lack of insurance drives folks in for the five o'clock special. And if you think the waiting area is insane, you should imagine what happens when the patients get into the rooms and confess why they are really there. Those in the waiting area are seen coughing, sneezing, a little vomit here or there, pain or some such and then there are those who don't seem to have any visible symptom. When each person wins a room the real tale or better fable comes out. Some are really there for birth control pills or an excuse to miss work for a headache that is already gone away so they say. To be fair, many are there for sincere reasons, just *not all*. Who knew part of the job would be to have "Judge Judy" like discernment for medical woes.

Now in urgent care and emergency rooms, patients are triaged or assessed to determine how soon they need to be seen. More emergent things are seen sooner than things such as colds, for instance. It would seem logical that if you are in the waiting room, having a soda, talking on your cell and just in from your cigarette, that you may wait a bit longer than say the elderly gentleman with chest pain, or the pale wheezing two year old. It might just be me, but this would seem to be expected, but no. Not everyone gets the higher priority of say, labor or a gunshot wound being slightly more urgent than the pain that began after Christmas three months ago. I am just thinking out loud.

Black Widow

As we sat at the desk we saw an adorable older lady approaching the counter of the urgent care. She wanted to be checked in for a bug bite. Her chart was sent back with no urgent priority. She seemed a little apprehensive, but did not verbalize any other complaints. When we went to triage her, we asked things like how long have you had the bite, when did you notice it. She looked up and said, "Well I am not sure how long I have had this but I noticed it when I went to pick up my nitroglycerin tablet. I had dropped it on the floor. I feel so silly" Now it is important to know that at that moment a thousand bells began ringing in my head at the word "nitroglycerin". Nitroglycerin, you see, is used for people who are having actual chest pain, the kind associated with heart attacks not the kind associated with anxiety like Moe earlier, yelling at your children or seeing your credit card bill. It was very clear that there might be another problem to consider.

We began to question her and found out she had taken three nitroglycerin pills and still had some chest pain but she really did not want to bother us with that. She knew we were busy and just wanted us to take a quick look at her bug bite. I convinced her that the bug bite could be seen much better in the treatment room, with her shirt off. "And as long as the shirt is removed what about a quick EKG (checks the heart activity) to see how you are doing?" I finally got her to agree and I was so glad. Within about fifteen minutes she was in an ambulance and on her way to the hospital for a possible MI (heart attack). As they were getting ready to put her in the ambulance she was still concerned about her bug bite. We assured her they would take care of that at the hospital. We see that a lot with our elderly folks, not wanting to be a burden. Very concerning to see so many endure symptoms or pain unnecessarily because they don't feel they are worth the time. THEY ARE. You ALL are.

"I'm not telling you it's going to be easy. I'm telling you it's going to be worth it." *Art Williams*

STEVE

Steve was a pleasant gentleman who was a "frequent flier". He made the rounds to every emergency room and urgent care in the valley. He would cycle through each one hoping to sell his story. Steve would come in for a dislocated shoulder, usually sobbing in pain. An x-ray was taken to confirm his complaint and sure enough, the shoulder was out of place. The physician would attempt to rotate it back in, Steve crying and screaming all the while. Usually a prescription for some pain medication would follow with the physician apologizing for causing so much distress. This particular night, however, his hand was called. He had gone to the pharmacy in the urgent care to fill the prescription.

The pharmacist had moonlit at another urgent

care two nights prior and had filled a rather generous prescription for the same narcotic for the same patient. He remembered this as he had thought the order a bit excessive at the time. And he remembered the shoulder story. His "crap-ometer" went into the red zone. He called back to the clinic to talk to the physician about his concern. The doc asked him to have the patient return for a moment.

The patient returned to the clinic, still looking convincingly in pain. The physician confronted him and let him know that he would not get his prescription that night and that his name would be sent through a central registry to all city pharmacies with his information on it. Steve stood up, started yelling, threw his shoulder back in place while throwing a mitt full of magazines with the "injured" arm then he stormed out of the clinic. We never saw him again.

SPECIAL DELIVERY

During a particularly quiet night a rather anxious lady came in to the clinic. She complained of stomach pain and nausea. During initial questioning she couldn't remember eating anything that upset her stomach, but she did know that she was going to the bathroom often. "As a matter of fact I had a huge accident earlier today soaking my pants. How crazy is that!" Information was passed on to the physician. A vaginal exam revealed some shocking news. She was delivering a baby, now! She initially denied it was possible. She swore she did not know she was pregnant. We assured her it was and she is!

Before the ambulance could arrive we had a second patient in the room. The baby arrived without event, fortunately, as urgent care centers are not equipped for crisis delivery situations. The baby cried on cue and so did the mother. We think it may have been for several reasons. Lesson learned: Never take wetting your pants for granted.

Mr. Pox

This finely dressed gentleman came into the emergency room on his way home from work. He was not sick, but he had developed a rash that seemed to spread over the course of a day. His employer required him to see a doctor before he could return to work. Like many men I know, he didn't have a doctor and hadn't seen one since his Pop Warner Football exam in high school. Well, as soon as the nurses saw him they suspected the worse and took him immediately to an exam room. The waiting room was scanned to see who shared his space.

A thorough head to toe exam revealed the horror. Chicken Pox. "Chicken Pox? I can't have chicken pox; I am thirty-seven years old." We assured him he could and did have them. Even worse, he would need to go home and remain quarantined for a few days. This was not pleasing news to him. And of course the patients that were exposed needed to be aware as well so they could minimize the risk of spreading to all their friends and family. This well put together man walked out shaking his head. He was not at all concerned about who may have been exposed. He was concerned that the guys at work would make fun of him for having a kid's disease. He could hear the prepubescent jokes flying across the office. We don't always give the preferred diagnosis but we try.

"I say to anyone considering a career in nursing: it is a demanding job, both physically and mentally. You will have to make sacrifices for the job, but the benefits are worth it." *- Heather L.,*

discovernursing.com

BOB

Now there is one thing that is essentially universal, the boss-staff relationship. Some are very interested in the wellbeing of their charges, others are completely oblivious to them. They have ideas which they are sure will improve everyone's work output. It is when the dawn of a new idea occurs that you find out which type of boss you have. One young man felt that if he saw a nurse sitting, they must be slacking off. Sitting equals non-productivity, lazy or wasteful right? OR it could (and in almost every case does) mean exhaustion, charting, planning, regrouping, even a desperate plea to the creator for one minute to pee. Or so this is how I remember it. And of course it may be the only three minutes the poor nurse sat down during their ten to twelve hour day, but he saw it therefore it was.

One day I decided to challenge him as he had

a fun side that I hoped would prevail. In this fast paced clinic setting there had to be full support. So I asked him to put on a lab coat and follow a nurse for the day. I guaranteed him that if he still felt the same way after his clinic adventure I personally would support his suggestions. He started out with his neat clothes and well groomed hair. Three sets of stitches, a urinary tract infection, a vomiting baby and a problem pregnancy later he took off the lab coat and promised to let us sit, undisturbed, whenever we got a chance. He lasted a full two hours.

POST FEAST

The holidays always bring in people that are sure they are dying. They complain of shortness of breath, horrible chest pain, pounding headache and bloating. Personally I am surprised that more people don't end up in the hospital for these complaints from simply enduring a family gathering. All that tension so little square footage. But I digress, so back to the emergency room. These patients are admitted to a room, striped down to their skivvies and hooked up to an EKG machine.

Once this is done and some careful questioning completed it is determined that until four thirty they were feeling fine. As a matter of fact, once the meal was finished the symptoms began. The traditional holiday meal report usually consists of three servings of cornbread dressing, two helpings of turkey, cranberry sauce, yams, rolls, green beans with fried onions and a piece of pumpkin pie with whipped cream. Oh yeah, there was also a boat of gravy. "And did I mention the summer sausage and cheese platter? I ate a lot of that before dinner?"

Indeed, a diagnosis is made, overeating! The antacids are given and yet another holiday has passed.

A standard discharge instruction would include simple advice like eat small portions, avoid fatty or fried foods, drink plenty of water, exercise, yada, yada. I am putting all my money on it, you have had that page for something and it didn't make it to your car. Two things you must know are important; chew your food and stop eating when you feel the only way to breathe is to loosen your pants.

BODY PIERCING

In the desert one must always be careful where they fall. Things like cactus are everywhere. During an afternoon hike a beautiful young girl fell face forward into a barrel cactus. She managed to miss her face but the thorns penetrated a large area of her chest. Poor girl, thirteen, who was now forced to bare her chest for someone with a magnifying glass and tweezers to pull the hundreds of thorns out of her chest that her family couldn't get out at home. She did really well with the whole process taking about three hours. The staff took turns looking and finding more of the fine, nearly invisible thorns. A chest x-ray was done and all felt confident we had succeeded.

Two nights later she returned with a fever and a possible infection. For the second time in as many days a room full of strangers was staring at her chest again. Nothing could be seen on visual assessment but the x-ray revealed an area of soft tissue inflammation. It was clear that some of the tiny needles had imbedded and were eluding detection. She was transferred to the hospital where they had to surgically remove the micro-fine cactus needle leaving her with a nice little scar and a healthy respect for botany. Curse you thorned enemy of the stumbled foot!

THE GOOD UNCLE?

Enter a man running and screaming at the top of his lungs, a little girl in his arms with blood covering her hair and face. The anxiety and fear was palpable. He kept saying, "I didn't mean to, it was an accident". Over and over he cried out for help, repenting for the tragic deed. Once we got him to stop spinning around, we were able to take the girl to the treatment room and get a better idea of the situation. She looked like she must have been scalped based on the blood. She was crying, completely freaked out would be more accurate, but with a little calm in the room we were able to get her to settle a bit. We washed off the bloody war paint to find a tiny two inch cut to the forehead.

Seems that the hysterical man was the girl's uncle and until tonight apparently did not know how tall he was. It was his first night babysitting his beloved niece and for fun he gave her a piggyback ride. Seems that the combination of their heights and a well-placed ceiling fan whirring silently above caused the head injury. As he galloped into the rotating blades a strong "whack" was heard and it all went red from there. It turned out that the small cut only needed a few steri-strip tapes and a Sesame Street Sticker. We gave him one too! Moral to this story, don't give piggyback rides in the house when the fans are on unless you are aware of the clearance.

ROMEO

There were some difficult cases, those that challenged your ability to treat all people compassionately despite their actions. One gentleman showed up for what he described as a cold. He did not exhibit any objective symptoms. He did seem nervous or antsy while waiting. Once he entered the exam room his story took a 180. I suspected it immediately when he did not want to divulge the true purpose of his visit. He began describing a whole nother set of issues that turned out to be a sexually transmitted disease he picked up in Mexico.

Apparently he did a bit more than conduct business of the moral kind while there. Symptoms began to develop that he knew were not going to be easy to explain. The physician told him it was bad but treatable. The patient was worried about going home to his wife and children. He didn't want them to catch something, of even greater concern; he didn't want to get caught with something. It was very hard to give those penicillin injections as gently as possible, but I did manage to refrain from injecting my personal judgment, so to speak. How many times we have to explain that the only way to avoid catching or experiencing things is to keep your pants on, wash your hands, don't share drugs, you know the list.

LIFE IN CRISIS

The critical care units are some of the most difficult whether it is in the neonatal unit or the trauma unit requiring high adrenaline, high emotion and a stretched mental load. Being tough is one of the hardest skills to master. My own father had a brief intensive care experience when he had his open-heart surgery. He was on the ventilator, just out of surgery which had us stressed to the max. He was trying to get my mom to understand something he was signaling with his fingers. Over and over again, until finally an epiphany occurred; he wanted a picture taken so he could see what he looked like. Who would know that would be on the mind of someone who has just had a massive heart attack and surgery. We got that picture but I believe my mother had some words first. It is amazing what a human thinks of in the midst of dying! Seriously!

The fact that he survived is miraculous in itself. You see in small towns doctors and operating rooms are not staffed 24/7. You usually have to call people in and wait for them to arrive. My father did not have that time. He had been in church, felt the pain but did not want to get up in the middle of the sermon. Grew up Baptist you see, suits and manners. So after the service concluded he told my mother she should probably take him to the hospital. When he arrived it just so happened that the cardiac cath lab nurse was working an extra shift in the emergency room and that the cardiovascular surgeon just happened to be making his daily rounds and just so happened that the O. R. had just finished an appendectomy. Everyone was in the hospital, everyone was in place. There is no doubt for me that Divine intervention occurred in this case. A gift for which we remained grateful until his last days.

"All of us must learn this lesson somewhere—that it costs something to be what we are."

Shirley Abbott (Zadra, 2003)

Sun

It was late one Friday night when the call came that we were getting a twenty year old in from a car accident. He had been ejected along with the driver. He was paralyzed from the neck down. He was handsome, a black belt in martial arts in his home country and an ambitious student. I received him the first night and followed him for the many weeks he was in the intensive care unit. Initially he experienced the usual sadness and anger, but several weeks on his back, unable to speak because of a ventilator and twenty-four hour noise he began to lose his sanity. It would take tough love and lots of patience to work him through this darkness.

He would click his tongue to get my attention, constantly. There was an evident fear of being unable to move and of being alone. I've got to tell you it was difficult at times to have him click constantly some nights as I tried so hard to figure out what he wanted or needed, if anything. Slowly he became more trusting of his bodies few remaining abilities and our commitment to care for him. Then there was the view, a grungy tile ceiling. That's it, all the noise around but the same limited view. I contacted our therapy department and got some prism glasses for him and his world opened up. These glasses have angled mirror that allows you to see a 90 degree view of the environment. He started getting acclimated to time, people and the reality he was in. By the time he was able to sit up he was much more comfortable with his changed world.

We all worked very hard to get him to think positive and to find some humor. By the time he left the unit someone had placed energizer bunny rabbits on his halo (the metal fitting that keeps the head and neck straight). He had a tracheotomy (opening in the throat) that he could cap and he learned to talk. He was able to tell some jokes and he had the greatest smile and laugh. He was going to be okay. He would end up living with a relative in town who was so kind and devoted to him. He was not shy about sharing how he became paralyzed and teaching others to avoid the same thing. I saw him a few years later and he was still the same handsome and motivated man. He had gone to college and done some public service bulletins related to seatbelt safety. I still see his wonderful smile. He took a life altering disability and turned it into his greatest ability!

"You must never so much think as whether you like it or not, whether it is bearable or not; you must never think of anything except the need, and how to meet it."

— *Clara Barton*

Henry

It was right at shift change we got the call that there was a twenty-six year old coming up from the ER, a self-inflicted gunshot victim. It was going to be one of those nights. I accepted the assignment. When the patient arrived he was intubated (on a ventilator), on I. V. drips and the consensus was he had been successful in his attempt. We were going to be waiting for the EEG results and the neurologist to come later on that night to let us know if there was any brain activity or not.

He was a nice looking man, round, tall with brown eyes. I got him settled and began the assessment and documentation process. The phone rang not long after and it was his wife calling from the hallway. When I got to a place where I was ready for her to come in, I pulled up a chair for her to sit in next to the bed. She looked twelve; in fact she was twenty-three. And so began the first long night. She told me the story of their life together that began when she was twelve. He was the only man she had ever loved, or dated for that fact. They married when she was seventeen and had five children.

He was a kind, hard-working man and happy with the children. But over the past year he had suffered from depression related mostly to the failure to advance at his job. He felt like he was failing the family and letting the children down. She had wanted to work, but he wanted her to be with the children.

The depression had gotten so bad that he had agreed to counseling and sought the help of a dear young pastor at a church near their home. He had seemed to be improving she thought.

This particular night he had planned to go out with some friends to a party. He had told them the party was outside of town near the lake. On the way there he asked them to stop so he could get something out of the trunk. The next thing they heard was a single gunshot. They got out only to find him lying on the road. He had planned it so that he would be out of earshot and out of sight from those he loved. The young friends were devastated.

As the night trickled on I learned about how they met, what the kids were like, about their friends and about their dreams. I encouraged her to talk about it all. I hoped she would be able to capture all the great memories of their life together in an effort to overshadow this horrible night. By the end of the night we knew what we expected, there was no brain activity revealed on the EEG and the recommendation was to turn off the life support and let him take the course ahead. She pulled the curtain after the doctor left and asked dozens of questions about what it all meant what would happen and what to expect after.

She asked me if I would be able to be there when it was time. I was already over shift time, but was scheduled to come back that night. She had a few people who needed to come by and say goodbye. Could it be done when I came back? Sure I told her. I felt like I had known them well myself after hearing the wonderful stories of their time together, and so I would be back to help with the next step.

After report that second night the first visitor arrived. It was that nice young pastor she had told me about. He told me about their talks and how he thought he had been able to help this man, but it seemed that he had failed. Suicide it seems causes everyone to have guilt even when it is unwarranted. I listened to him talk about his time with this couple, how he had prayed for him and how he had hoped for him. I assured him he had not failed because he had been faithful in his efforts to give him another way and to intercede on his behalf. That is all we can do sometimes, I said, is hope. Each person is still responsible for his or her final choices.

I felt led to tell him what I have come to believe over the years in this profession. You do not know when they have their last thought nor can you tell what it is. While this was a tragic event, we would not know what his thoughts were about God, his family or when he had that thought. All we would know is that for him, this was the only answer he could act on, and it was his way of trying to provide more for his family. Had he had a chance to think through what they would be missing, he would probably have changed his mind, but it is not a rational thought that commits this act. The pastor seemed to feel some relief and went back out to be with the family.

Finally the wife came in, she was ready. We pulled the curtain and I encouraged her to talk to him, tell him all the things she had to say and hold his hand. She thanked him for loving her and for all their beautiful children. She told him how much she had loved every minute together. Then she sat quiet for a time. She called me in and we were ready. I turned the ventilator off and I saw her eyes well up. I reached over to put my arm around her and she hugged me tightly. We sat there for some time, hugging and crying. I will never forget that time. She had not looked at him since the ventilator was turned off. When she was finally ready to go, she looked at me and asked if she should look back. I asked her what picture she had in her mind and she described the nice round warm face that had come in. I told her to keep that memory and turned the lights down so she would not see the change of color and appearance he had once the ventilator was off. I walked her out and we said our good-byes.

While there are many happy times I have memories of, it is the times like these that remain. These are the times when nurses become most vulnerable and often become a part of a life we would otherwise have missed. And even if it was for a short time, I will always feel a part of this life and all the good memories he left behind.

"Through the centuries we faced down death by daring to hope." *Maya Angelou (Zadra, 2005)*

James

One thing you learn quickly in the intensive care unit is that those who come in under the influence will need to be restrained. It is them or you, literally. When people come down from the artificial high, they are known to be violent. I have learned more four-letter words from these folks then I ever learned in high school. As a matter of fact I believe there are pages of the dictionary missing. Then there is the behavior, obscene or violent. A nurse has to be constantly aware of two things with this group, medical changes and personal risk. The beautiful thing to remember is that once these folks are free of their demons their true selves come out and most of the time they are fine people. They benefit from patience and encouragement to find their potential.

One man was a frequent flier. Alcoholic and some drug addictions. He was in his forties and regularly was found in a coma on some street. The sad thing for him is the heartache he caused his parents. Time and time again they would receive a call from an emergency room or police station that this man claimed to be their son. Did they want to come in? Did they have funds to help him? Would they take him home? Many nurses are faced with their own beliefs or limited view of situations such as this. Some would criticize that the parents would not come in or give him money. The patient would tell us stories about his circumstance.

What we came to learn later was that this man had been given money, housing, treatment, and jobs yet still continued in his lifestyle. He had even broken in to his parent's home and stolen to support his lifestyle. He chose this path and his parents were forced to make tough decisions as a result. It was tough love at its most challenging and painful point. They never gave up hope that one day their son would overcome and be freed of the empty and dangerous life he chose. In the meantime they had to hope from a distance. A constant reminder not to judge what you do not know. There is always so much more than we know or see. And it is often at great price.

"You really can change the world if you care enough." *Marian Wright Edelman (Zadra, 2005)*

Sam

One patient weighed in at eight hundred pounds or so. A special bed was brought in for him so he could be cared for safely and be comfortable. Besides addressing his medical needs, this patient was placed on a strict weight loss diet. Things started out good, but after a couple of weeks the weight stopped falling off. It would be one night while looking for a medical device that we found the cause. Ding Dongs, lots of them. And some Milky Way bars.

Apparently mom felt so bad about us starving her child that she had been bringing in food and hiding it all around the bed. We asked the patient how he felt about his health and whether or not he wanted to lose weight. He really did want to lose weight but felt too weak or defeated to do it. The nurses assured him that they would help him at least while he was in the hospital and would help him find resources when he was discharged.

With his approval his mom's visits were restricted and supervised from that day forward. All furniture was inspected after every visit as well. Those parents who are of the old school of "food means love", you need an updated course. Excessive eating and junk foods mean clogged arteries, horrible quality of life and likely an early death. Flowers, jewelry or a ball of some kind are good alternatives. Love your family, lock the cupboard!

Al Capone, Jr?

So the worst nightmare a nurse can experience is gun violence in the unit. Well, we 'lived' through the closest thing, a full-fledged gang fight. After a gang fight on the street left two individuals wounded, one was admitted directly to the intensive care unit while the other was admitted to the surgical floor. As the patient in the unit began to improve, it was decided to transfer him to the floor.

As he was rolled out of the unit, walking up the hall was another patient. What we did not know until that moment was that he was the one who had tried to take out our guy. The one walking up the hall suddenly flashed his gang sign at his homies (I am not all that but you get my drift) and hollered at his guys in the waiting room to go get the rest of the gang. And the fight began, just like that.

Before it was done there were broken chairs, tables, windows and bones! Several staff attempted to separate the gangs and they were assaulted in the process. Security and police were called and eventually ended the battle. The hospital was locked down for several weeks, which meant the patients in question were separated and placed in units that had secure doors. It is not likely that when you think of a nurse you think of a life-threatening gang war profession, but here it is, case and point. It is not just dishing up bedpans and medications.

In this particular area of town there was a gun battle on many occasions. There was a heavy fire event outside our front door about 6 a.m. one day.

The time nurses come to work. Most just parked their cars and walked in as they assumed they were not the targets. The gunfire eventually stopped. A bullet was noted to be lodged firmly between the two panes of glass in the CEO's office window. Other than that, it was business as usual.

Ruth

Ruth was a middle aged woman with multiple issues who spent her last several months in the intensive care unit. She was frail, in her early sixties, and had fragile bones from her rheumatoid arthritis. She was in critical condition and her prognosis was extremely grave. The physicians spent hours talking to her about whether or not being resuscitated, having chest compressions done should her heart stop, was a good idea. The fear was one compression and her bones would snap and death would be certain.

She on the other hand was terrified to die and

felt that even if every bone broke; taking that chance to live was paramount. Spiritual care had visited and despite a lovely conversation it did not provide her any comfort in death or the afterlife. And as expected, she did arrest (her heart and breathing stopped) and at the first chest compression every bone cracking could be heard as well as cartilage breaking apart. It became gruesome from there. She suffered additional bleeding and the entire attempt was unsuccessful. Not one of us wanted to perform CPR on this patient and none of us could get the sound out of our heads for quite some time. We did not feel successful in this life.

"How very little can be done

under the spirit of fear"

Florence Nightingale: British Nurse and

Humanitarian. 1820-1910

Manuel

Manuel was admitted to the trauma unit with internal bleeding. His condition was critical and he needed surgery right away. The surgeon was talking to the family about the risks and attempting to obtain consent for the procedure including blood transfusion should he need it. "Absolutely not! It is a forbidden thing. We are Jehovah's Witness." That put the brakes on for several minutes. The physician had the same detailed conversation with the patient and he said he would take a transfusion if needed while the wife argued with him telling him he must refuse. This patient was being forced to choose life or death based on his convictions.

The patient fully competent told the physician to perform the surgery and do whatever was needed. He just wanted to be able to see his grandchildren grow up. After the yelling subsided, the family left.

They told him that if he died it would be God's judgment on him for taking blood. They didn't stay, they didn't call to check on him and they never came back. He had a large family and spent every waking moment speaking very kindly about them, even after they walked out. He was not angry at them. He just wanted to live. We talked throughout that night.

The surgery went well and when he returned from recovery he was awake and amazingly alert. He began to reminisce. He talked about his family, growing up, his own children and his life in general. I enjoyed hearing the many wonderful stories he shared about his younger days, his marriage and his children. But reminiscing is something most nurses don't like to see. It is an eerie thing, a sixth sense perhaps. It would almost appear that folks who do this know they are about to pass and want to relive a few memories.

And just like that, he had an unfortunate change in status and ended up dying before the shift ended.

This man's desire was to be with his family. I don't believe it was a judgment by God, but his family did and passed their judgment. They did not return nor did they claim his body. They never said goodbye. I spent many days in sadness. I have never understood.

"It was not my strength that wanted nursing, it was my imagination that wanted soothing."

— *Joseph Conrad, Heart of Darkness*

THE DAILY GRIND

Most of the hospitals general floors are comprised of hallways of rooms filled with stories of every kind. The trend is now to have single rooms but in older facilities and the days gone by there may have been two to four in a room. People could be in for the slightest affliction in the old days or a terminal illness, all sharing space and staff and time. Nothing happens two days in a row the same. NOTHING! Except my coffee, black and lots of it.

A LITTLE SUGAR

It was a very quiet night and well after midnight so everyone had settled into their chairs for a bit of quiet time before rounds. Suddenly and simultaneously a nurse call light rang out and there was a blood curdling scream. Staff flew out of their chairs, papers and books flying everywhere. They arrived on the scene to find this precious, fragile elderly lady *not alone* and in a bit of distress. It seems that an elderly man, suffering from Alzheimer's, had gotten up and had wandered into the wrong bed. He had crawled in and was having a little snuggle. This was not his wife however, and this dear lady clearly did not want any company.

It took several minutes to calm everyone down, but eventually we got each one in to their respective beds. He could not understand why 'his' girl did not let him stay. He earned a companion to monitor his room after the mishap. As for the traumatized woman, I don't know that she ever turned off her room light again during her hospital stay. While it is a humorous situation for us, it is also a sad thing to see our beautiful elders disappear into the past. I watched both my parents experience this to some level. The joy I had was that they were both happy in their memories for the most part. So while they did not always know me, they knew someone just like me or thought they would like to. That was good enough for me.

CALLING ALL HANDS

What do you do when a patient falls out of bed? Call the fire department, or at least that is what it took to get one patient back to bed. She was a very nice and completely embarrassed 998-pound patient we needed to get back to bed. She had been trying to adjust her bed so that it would go from a lying position to a chair position. Her goal was she could stand up from the foot of the bed. And by all sound judgment it should have worked as she was in a special bed to accommodate her and keep her comfortable.

Well, concept great, slippery fabric, bad! As the head came up and the foot went down gravity took over and she slid straight out the bottom. Despite several willing and able bodied staff, they were not enough to get this dear Lady back to bed. She had just wanted to get up for a walk! Six hard bodied firemen and nine nurses later we were successful in reaching the mattress with our charge. It is at times such as these that many of us evaluate the condition we are in and are inspired to take measures to avoid such a situation in our own lives. God Bless Firemen!!

UNEXPECTED GUESTS

A wound care nurse will occasionally get stat calls. But as a wound care specialist, there is really not a need for a "stat" consult since most wounds are developed over time and aren't going to heal any differently. One day, I received a stat call from the emergency room, and less than five minutes later from the geriatric unit and then immediately after that from the nurse on that floor. My pager was going off like mad as well. I arrived to the unit to see the staff in full PPE (personal protective equipment). I walked to the room and they offered to dress me likewise. Of course I inquired, "What is in there that requires a gown, mask, hat, shoe covers and two pair of gloves"? I declined all but ONE pair of gloves.

I walked over to the patient to observe a small wound on his foot, about two inches across. Not too bad for a wound, of course there were also small white 'tentacle' like projections wiggling in the wound. LOTS of them! They were maggots that had nested in the wound. And the staff was certain that the little uninvited guests would dive or hop or fly onto the nearest body. Not to worry, as I sense you are, but maggots don't flip, fly or jump. They are quite happy in their little home and won't leave unless driven out. That would be my job. Once the patient was freed from the demon beasts, the staff found they were able to resume their daily tasks. They eventually quit scratching, squirming and making the 'eww' sound. Important lesson; know your pests and dress accordingly.

SALLY

Violence comes in all forms and at any age. Those who think nursing is a cushy job really have not paid attention to some of the better medical dramas. In this area they are not all that far off. Life happens in all forms and levels of intensity. We really should consider hazard pay some (most) days. One very memorable event was at the hands of an elderly woman, in her late eighties. She was confused, and combative. She had soiled her bed and was in desperate need of a clean-up. We had to gather the helpers and the necessary linen to accomplish a full body wash. It (yes brown IT!) was everywhere.

Her arms and legs were flailing everywhere. As we were attempting to clean her she suddenly reached up and pinched my neck, full force with her thumb and fingers effectively clamping off the main vessel in my neck, then she twisted it. I got dizzy and nearly hit the floor. It seemed a bit long to me but the other nurses managed to get the tightly clamped fingers off my neck. I took several minutes to recover but did eventually get myself back in the game. Late eighties my foot! I would guess that those self-defense classes for the nursing home staff are quite advanced. I left the room completely impressed, and somewhat light headed. And I gained a lot of respect for the power of 80!

BREAST CANCER

Often I have been faced with caring for women with breast cancer. It affects everyone somewhere somehow. It affects a family member, relative or friend. Seeing patients admitted with cancer is not as surprising as the fact that some of them wait until the breast is hard, enlarged or even open and sore. Seeing patients come in at later stages of disease is a challenge. Cancer that is not caught and treated early can decrease options or eliminate them completely. Some say they wait as they are embarrassed to get a checkup or tell their spouses or they are afraid of dying.

Culture is a big factor for many who do not seek help. It is not acceptable to get female exams because of some belief or law. The families will not support the woman being gone from the home and children for treatments. Some don't have the money or resources and don't know how to find them. I personally am impacted by patients, family and friends who have endured, beaten or lost to breast cancer. Seeing the global impact of this disease has been one of the great motivators for me to get an annual mammogram and commit to the Susan G. Komen Race for the Cure and the 3 day 60 mile breast cancer walk. Most breast cancer patients are great fighters and extremely inspirational. They share insight into the value of life every day and remind me every day not to grumble about the little aches and pains.

I have dozens of stories, real life stories that have shown me the resilience of individuals that have faced cancer, determined to do what was necessary and remained hopeful. From diagnosis to that first 'cancer free' scan, emotions of all kinds are experienced. I have held hands, prayed, cried, hugged and been the goof ball that I am most skilled at being to distract from the nausea or yucky taste of food to admiring the brand new, never gonna sag breast. It is really a team effort starting with the patient and their creator and collecting the team along the journey.

Then there are those like a dear patient who hid her cancer out of shame until she could not take the odor any more. It was open, advanced and caused her to lose her appetite and her family to shun her. I had a couple of staff who made audible remarks or gasps due to the odor that I pulled aside to remind them of her burden. I was able to utilize some special dressings on the outside that eliminated the odor that previously could be smelled down the hall. She ate. She tolerated her meds. And we worked with the charity clinic and the company to help her get more so that her life that was left would allow her to be in the company of her family and friends. I spent a lot of time with her while she was there. She was 31. She was beautiful to me in every way. Ww5.komen.org

"The bravest sight in all this world is someone fighting against the odds."

Franklin Lane (Zadra, 2003)

YOU WANT ME TO GO WHERE??

Seriously, home health is extremely

dangerous. Sending individuals into people's homes in all corners of the earth armed with an iPad and a cell phone. And when I say homes I use the word in its most eclectic sense. There are tiny homes, homes on wheels, mansions, apartments, trailer's, tents, parks and shelters. And some of them look like they belonged in a horror movie from the lack of lighting to the freaking herd of barking dogs! But, we smile, grab our Mary Poppins medicine kit and off we go.

ARMED AND DANGEROUS

Directions are critical when working in home health. One wrong turn and you can end up anywhere. One of my favorite directions were as follows: Take the freeway seven miles south of the bridge, turn right at the convenience store, turn left at the dead dog then right at the pig skull. The patient would be waiting in his sweat lodge just past the snakeskin. Sure enough the dog, the skull and the snakeskin were there as was the sweat lodge.

There is no preparation for "scary" in nursing school. Nor do they give nursing students a weapons review manual. One patient was confined to a bed, partially paralyzed from the neck down as a result of a gunshot wound, 'partially' being the operative word here. Apparently he had some bad habits that required drug dealing and firearms. He had a large pressure ulcer (bed sore) that the home health was caring for. I rang the doorbell and after a considerable wait was permitted to enter the dimly lit room.

I walked into his room to see skull and cross bones on the wall and he was listening to some pretty loud, hostile sounding music. I turned him over to inspect the offended backside only to discover a shotgun, sawed off, lying at his side. I asked him why, a paralyzed man with limited arm function would pack such a "piece" and he said he has had gang fights at his home and he liked to be prepared. Gang fights? Shotguns? In his home? Last will and testament? When I finished, I informed him I would come back when he wasn't armed and had a lock on the door.

Packing heat is not just for the young at heart I came to find out. A seventy-five year old woman slept with a machete under her pillow. She lived in a poor section of town and had been the victim of a number of break-ins. "If they think they can get me without a fight, they will think again. Last time I gutted him like a dead deer." I assured her I would knock loudly and come at the same time each day so she would not mistake me for a deer! I still am not sure if she was kidding or not. Was not going to find out.

Life Long Friend

One hazard or blessing when you are in home health is that you may have your patients for years. You get to know them and their families intimately. Some may have things you never want to know though they are eager to tell you every detail. Others you hope you never have to discharge because they are such a joyful part of your life. One such family I adopted and I still have contact with today. He had cancer and fought well for several years. He was a military man with a beautiful wife. They had a passion for living and each other. It was a truly beautiful relationship. He had stories upon stories from his military days and happy married days he shared with his wife, a retired military nurse.

His wound is what brought me there, but his heart is what kept me coming. His wife was the same. And being a military brat, I could enjoy both the military stories and their many adventures. My father had experienced most of the same things, as he was only two or three years behind my friend. He would eventually lose his fight, succumbing to cancer. His wife and I have remained close and she became one of my closest friends. They were a gift and it is encounters such as these that keep a nurse going. They build you up and remind you why you went into a service industry such as nursing.

HAVE CELL PHONE WILL TRAVEL

Danger is always in the back of your mind when you do home health. You are going to every corner of town and into homes of complete strangers. You never know what you will encounter, human or otherwise. As I agreed to go on one visit they said a "by the way" remark. This should have given me great pause, but being young and carefree I ventured out to the remote home anyway. The "by the way" for this visit was that three women lived in this trailer. It would be of note that their spouses were all in prison for murdering and butchering a woman making a delivery a few years earlier.

Great! I would like to tell you I am brave, but I walked up to the door with my cell phone in one hand and a jumbo pepper spray in the other. So that you appreciate the magnitude of my self-defense, in those days the cell phone was the size and weight of a brick, so it would have been effective if I needed to strike a defensive blow, or so I assure myself even today. Of course there was not a single bar to my service in this isolated area, so it would have been its only purpose as I entered the property. Once I decided that I was not going to be at risk I was able to complete my duties and leave quickly!! It so reminded me of the days I cared for patients in the county jail or prison. I would rather not know 'why' they are there just 'what' they need me for. TMI!!!

SNAKE?

Nonhuman threats come in all forms. One place I made several visits to would hardly be called a house by even poverty standards. I had to announce my arrival at the gate so they could lock up the three pit bulls who I was assured had only bitten a couple of times before. Then I would go through the "curtain" which hung over the outside doorframe of what used to be the door to visit the patient directly inside. The patient was partially paralyzed, into dungeons and dragons and had a number of occult symbols around the room. The music was loud, eerie and dark, the only thing missing was a bong and its aroma. I grew up in the seventies.

One day as I was assessing the huge opening in the hip, I heard a rustling noise. I paused, cocked my ear and then continued. It happened several times and I was finally overcome with curiosity so I asked what that rustling noise might be. "Oh don't worry," he said with a grin, "it is probably just a mouse." I moved my feet back from the edge of the bed about a foot so I could at least get a visual if the critter decided to run up my pant leg. It was then that the patient laughed and said "You don't have to worry; my snake usually gets them right away." "Snake??" "Oh yeah, he lives under the bed." You just never know where danger lives.

GETTING A VISUAL ON REAL LIFE

Home health nursing also allows you to see how people live. Most people live fairly ordinary lives, while some may surprise you. An attorney living in a huge home had one of the filthiest homes I had ever seen inside, feces on the floor, garbage everywhere and sinks that looked like they should be condemned. But he sure looked neat and tidy for court in his suit. Another home had birds that were flying free, droppings everywhere. On the opposing end was a woman who lived in one of the most immaculate, grandest homes. I am talking 15,000 square feet of designer living, every room with a view. Yet this lady never left her bed. It is not that she couldn't it is that she wouldn't. She even had a bedsore from the lack of effort she would make to move. She had people come to clean, shop and cook and essentially they occupied her home while she never left her bed. All that wealth and no joy. Money is not all it is cracked up to be, and that I saw over and over again. I saw many who had none and were the most at peace.

Sometimes folks think that because you are a nurse you can diagnose and treat everything, including the dog. One house, located left of the burnt tree and one mile past the dead lizard had a dog with mange (dog scabies). After I saw the patient, the family brought the dog into the one room house and asked if I could treat the dog while I was there. I assured them that even I had limitations and a veterinarian may be the way to go, or at least a pet supply store. I want to make it clear, we are nurses, not doctors, not pharmacists and we are not allowed to diagnose and treat. I say this knowing that it will not stop neighbors, family or you from calling to ask for medical advice. You know it's true.

Some patient's don't live in houses; they live in campers or in parks. It can be a little awkward to try to find your contact in a park with ten people or in a campground. One patient said he would make it easy, as his camper was too small to stand in, so he would wait for me outside. "You will know me. I will be the one sitting in a chair and showing my legs." Sure enough as I drove around I saw him sitting there in a folding chair with his pant legs pulled up to his knees. Worked for me! I did his complete visit right there in the sunlight. A good nurse is always flexible, able to go with the flow, adapt to any situation, or can at least throw a smile on and fake their way through.

I had the privilege to meet several holocaust survivors. Most of them were in their late seventies to early nineties. Those that would speak about it had horrific stories of torture, death and survival. Amazingly they harbored very little hatred. I was so impressed at their ability to live through such terrible circumstances yet still be able to move forward. From the many recollections I was privileged to hear, the movies and documentaries can hardly do justice to those daily events in the camps and the deep fear that hung over them every minute. It is an honor to provide a small service to someone who suffered greatly and who has lost so much.

"Nursing is a kind of mania; a fever in the blood; an incurable disease which, once contracted, cannot be got out of the system. If it was not like that, there would be no hospital nurses, for compared dispassionately with other professions, the hours are long, the work hard, and the pay inadequate to the amount of concentrated energy required. A nurse, however, does not view her profession dispassionately. It is too much a part of her." — *Monica Dickens*

Margaret

There is a frequent question that haunts every nurse: What do you do when you are asked to take care of a patient who will do nothing to improve their situation? We see this over and over in every care setting. Margaret was a diabetic with sores to her lower leg and she insisted that we need to make it better; all the while she is smoking two plus packs a day, dropping ashes all over her legs leaving huge burns. A case worker evaluated her home setting to find she lived alone, is blind, has numerous pets and no resources.

During her treatment she eats only junk and sugar, her blood sugar is in the four hundreds all the time (ideal is less than 120) and she hasn't had a bath in weeks. She refuses any attempts to provide hygiene from staff. The pets have left hair everywhere including her wounds. When she is at home the risk for fire alone is incredible as she has dropped hot ashes on the carpet resulting in hundreds of burn marks. These are the cases that leave you feeling helpless, there is nothing you can do to make this person choose to make changes or desire to live better.

The nurse fails in these cases, not because they want to but because there are no options. This is health care's Kobayashi Maru, the Star Trek test that cannot be won unless Captain Kirk reprograms the test, changing the test condition and cheats death. If only that scenario could play out in real life. In general they become highly charged, emotional experiences with protective services, family conflict and anger. Because we care we have to endure this more often than you know.

SHARED STORIES

Every nurse has a few hundred (thousand) stories to share. There is probably not enough paper to contain them all even if we took out the entire rain forest. The stories vary from hilarious to utter sadness. They range from the neonate (preemie) to the geriatric (elderly) patient. The common thread is upon hearing a tale we are reminded of fifty more just like them. And they all involve a patient, a nurse and a situation from which to grow. Here are just a few that have stuck with me.

THE EYES HAVE IT

A young nursing assistant was bathing a patient. She was a very thorough assistant and the patient would be clean as a whistle when she was done. She was also very superstitious which the patient knew. As the assistant was washing her patient, the patient popped out her eye (don't panic, it was artificial) and said, "Could you wash this too while you are at it?" The poor assistant ran off screaming. It took several minutes and lots of talking to get her back in the room. The patient gleefully agreed to keep her eyes to herself.

LAST CHRISTMAS

A mother of three young children was diagnosed with a rare form of cancer, it was terminal. She was not a citizen so there were a million issues the most important being that her children would miss Christmas as she was in the hospital and had no more money. Her two young single brothers were going to take on the task of raising the kids, but they themselves were migrant workers with minimal resources. It was if there was no hope. But the word spread quickly among the staff and physicians resulting in an enormous last Christmas for this mom to share with her family and some relief for what she was about to leave behind. It is my understanding that Christmas was delivered anonymously to this family every year until the youngest turned 18.

WIFE?

One older gentleman was walking down the hall when he noticed a female patient walking towards him. They were each doing there required "laps" or walk as part of the recovery after their heart surgeries. He started to chat with her, and it was clear he found her attractive. As they continued to talk, he told her that she looked exactly like his third wife, her hair, and the beautiful eyes. On and on he went clearly on a roll. She couldn't help herself, she had to know. "How many times have you been married?" she asked. "Twice" he said with a twinkle in his eye. A good chuckle was had. I still wonder if he got her to say yes.

A 'SLIDE' OF HAND

A gentleman with Alzheimer's would sometimes become quite confused and agitated. He would become aggressive with staff and visitors at times as well. One day while the nurse was trying to change his linen he leaned forward and bit down hard on the hand of the nurse. Out of shear reaction, the nurse pulled the hand back and to her surprise and relief, the teeth came with it and flew across the room. She was free. The dentures were miraculously not damaged in the incident and the nurse left with a complete set of fingers.

SPECIALIZED SPECIALTY OR WHAT DO I DO NEXT?

I found myself in a nursing field that happened completely by accident. I had been working in the trauma unit on nights for a year and a half. I was emotionally and physically tired and really wanted a change. The enterostomal therapist position was open. This type of nurse works with patients who have colostomies, ileostomies, urostomies and other types of tubes and openings; things that smell bad and drain. I had a long history working with patients with ostomies and was given the Monday through Friday day job. What a treat. I began reading the literature and journals related to the profession and I became fascinated with wounds and the care of all types of injuries. It remains my first passion!

I was privileged to be working under a physician who is internationally recognized for his expertise in wound management. He has published chapters in books, articles and presented to audiences around the world. He is a faculty at the medical university as well. He was completely supportive and literally put wings under my feet. I have worked as a wound care specialist for twenty five years now and it has been a great experience. I have been involved in research, product development, teaching, writing articles, a book chapter and speaking at conferences around the country. It has been an unexpected joy and always fascinating. I am continually grateful for his support and ongoing friendship to this day.

And yet it is a very tiny part of the large and glorious world of nursing. Nurses specialize in dozens of areas. Research is an area that helps to determine not only what we do, but also how we do it. It tests new ways to use old practices and new practices to give better results. It can include medications, procedures, equipment, processes and more. As far as the imagination can go, that's where research can take you. These nurses spend countless hours reading charts, collecting data and attempting new or better ways to provide care to the patient. The money and time involved in trialing and approving the smallest item can be staggering. But when it improves the outcome for even one individual it is worth it all. One unusual research question led to a rather interesting rabbit hole you can enjoy in the addendum.

Then there are neonatal nurses. They work with babies that are born early or small. They may care for babies at just under a pound and provide the babies and their families with a glimmer of hope for a future. They may have these babies for days or months and they give heart and soul to getting them prepared to go home. They dress them in tiny cloths and provide them with little toys and warm fuzzy things. They give medications in such small amounts that they are almost unmeasurable, but they do it with precision. They talk to them, sing to them and touch them gently. They help their families to see that the tiny package that cannot yet be held is a beautiful human waiting to grow up.

Community health nurses are all about you in

your neighborhood. I have met numerous creative and driven creatures who thrive on getting the care to where the needs are. This often may take them away from their homes for days and require them to write for grants to support ideas or to propose big projects to companies or government. They actually fight, scratch and claw to take care of those in the most desperate need even if they are gone for weeks at a time or have to live in a trailer.

One gal had a heart for teenagers. She felt many were not seeking any help or guidance from physicians or families resulting in high teen pregnancy and sexually transmitted diseases. She created the idea for a mobile clinic that would be at certain schools each week. Hundreds of teens found her a supportive friend and resource. In several schools there were documented significant decreases in teen pregnancies and disease.

Another community nurse practitioner developed a mobile medical unit and drove to the outlying areas and reservations across the state providing immunizations, physicals and prevention services. She was away from her home often two to four weeks at a time as the schedules filled up in these remote regions. It is fascinating to think that a nurse meets a need as simple as this and even more concerning that the need still exists in 2015 America.

Free clinics are another place nurses can be found. They often volunteer, their only pay being the smile and appreciation of the individuals they serve. The Catholic Church sponsors one such clinic in our community. They provide medical care and dental care to those who have no insurance and or no income. Every item they use is donated by companies and individuals. They see everything from broken fingers to asthma to heart disease and diabetes. It is a cross-cultural group so they see folks that don't speak English, have different cultural issues and lifestyles than we would typically deal with. These folks have to be well versed in a number of diverse areas. A diabetic diet to an American is completely different than that of someone of European or Hispanic descent. Creative patient education is their greatest challenge and they are incredible at it.

There are too many specialties to list. But it is important to know that in most cases these nurses have chosen to leave the traditional nursing role. They have had extra specialized educational training and may have had to take extra licensing or certification exams to perform their craft. They may have had to go back to school to get a higher degree even before they could consider a specialized career. They have taken extra steps to bring more advanced care to the patient and to share that knowledge with the nursing staff. All of which improves the potential outcome for our patients.

FINAL THOUGHTS

So there you have it, a glimpse of the nursing life. A nurse is that human whose hands will clean you, provide medication for you and comfort you. Understanding nurses and the job they do will help in developing expectations and understanding the next time you seek care. Nurses are not there just to serve your family coffee but to help you, the patient! They are all about helping you to get well and hopefully go home. In any given shift they will see life and death side by side. They will try to put on the brave front as they walk in to each room, but will be affected by it all just the same.

Can you imagine going to a neighbor's house

to watch their grandmother die one minute and then go to another neighbor's house to have cheesecake? Most days are like that as the nurse walks down the hall from one room to the next. That may be why some nurses may seem distant or detached. They are often trying to process and move on from another situation on the other side of your door. Will you be the deathbed or the cheesecake?

Then there are the visitors. Your needs are important to that nurse as are the needs of the others under their charge but consider the number of issues and requests that visitors can bring in to the hospital setting. If each patient has two visitors a day, that nurse now has three times as many personalities and issues to deal with. It is not that visitors are bad; they are usually a welcome distraction for the patient and nurse. But that is not always the case. The nurse ends up caring for their patients in addition to whatever the family demands may encompass. It might be interesting for you to think that you may be the nicest person the nurse is dealing with at a particular time! They do it because they care. While they will try to satisfy the demands of a large number of people during a shift they ultimately want to see that their patients are receiving what they need.

One thing is an absolute for the nurse, change is expected and it is constant. Contracts change so the products they used last week are not there now and they need to find what has replaced it. Research will dictate that something they have done for years is now outdated. What was good last year is not good today. Units are remodeled, computer programs are changed, forms are created or eliminated, policies are revised, and it goes on and on. It is like every day you have to look for your socks because your sock drawer has been moved, again! The only constant in the healthcare profession is change.

Some nurses will not be natural conversationalists. They love what they do but gab is not their gift. If their skills are good and the outcome is good, less chat may be okay. This group often seems to be the group that will be accused of being rude, failing to respond appropriately or they respond in a way that may be offensive. Though this small group has a sincere desire to help their fellow human; they are just not gifted with some of the social skills. They are like that checker at the grocery store, the one who does not make eye contact or greet you. She still rings up your groceries and gives you the correct change, but without the pleasantries that we find appealing. In some cases, the lack of chatter may be the nurses' way to protect them self from what they see each day.

What they see is not exclusive to the healthcare job either. They suffer 'life' when they are away from you. They have depression, anger, loneliness, marital discord, loss of children, personal illness or disease and any number of other events occurring. For some work also provides an escape form unbearable things at home while others seem to be more affected by the life cycle they see at work. Appreciate that you, by entering their care, have become a piece of their life story. They will remember you in one way or another.

Nurses spend more time at work in a given day then they do with their own families. They literally spend twelve or thirteen plus hours with you, your family and your roommates or next-door neighbors. They give their entire waking day to total strangers. In most cases it is more time than they will give to their families on their days off. Balance is a very difficult task for a nurse; they are challenged to not give so much at work that they are too tired or emotionally drained to give at home. And the surprising thing is they usually don't mind. They are there because they want to be. They want to take care of the sick, stubborn and dying. How many people do you know that want to get up in the morning or stay up all night to do that? It is all about you.

It is important to remember that the nurse is not the reason you are in the hospital. It is your health that brings you in and often that is related to the choices you made during your lifetime. We are all subject to the consequences of our decisions; nurses are not excluded. Patients become angry with the nurse because they are not allowed to have chocolate cake at lunch because of their diabetes, and yet it is not the nurses' fault the patient has diabetes, or that their blood sugar was out of control and they had to be hospitalized. In most cases it is that lifestyle that will bring us all to the care of others.

I guarantee if you consider the commission of the nurse to selflessly care for others, and the emotional weight they carry, you will look at them in a different light. The expectations you have for them might change, not in the level of care you should receive but perhaps in the manner in which that care arrives. You may even come to realize that despite every legal firm ad assuring you that all your problems are someone else's fault, the nurses did not cause you to come to them and they did the best they could with the hand you dealt them. It is a truth even a nurse has to admit. We all arrive at the doctors' office or hospital door with the same need. That is the need for someone to care for us. The nurse has made a choice too. They chose to care and they will care for us all at some point in time. And they will do their best as for them it is truly more than a job.

"I think one's feelings waste themselves in words;

they ought all to be distilled

into actions which bring results."

Florence Nightingale: British Nurse and

Humanitarian. 1820-1910

Addendum

TAMING OF THE LOO

My search for the creator of the urinal has taken me on an obscure and fascinating journey to labs and countries around the world. While I was unable to determine exactly who the inventor of the urinal was I did discover some interesting facts such as who made the bedpan pretty and where the loo began way down under.

From the centuries of written articles and practice reports, it was evident that people have urinated in any number of objects made of a variety of materials including wood, plastic, metal, porcelain, polyurethane and glass. For example, the flushing toilet was invented by John Harrington in 1596 and the first practical water closet by Joseph Bramah of Yorkshire, England in 1778.

In prisoner of war camps in Thailand, supplies for the prisoners were not provided leaving the outdoor sanctuary for most of their bodily functions. However in the infirmary beds they were provided bedpans crafted of large bamboo (Duncan, 1983). While bamboo is an attractive wood source, I had a difficult time envisioning it under my precious and most sensitive behind.

It would be the Canadians who would focus on beautifying the bedpan and urinal. In 1873 the St. Johns Stone Chinaware Company was founded and it lasted until the turn of the century. They were famous for their tableware and ultimately their toilet ware. Hmm, it is an interesting production concept. They created the white simple porcelain receptacles and decorated them with the thin blue trim (Civilization, 2005). Certainly style is an important consideration when envisioning where to relieve ones' self.

One significant thing that was proved by science in the early part of the 20th century was the fact that things do grow in bedpans. It was in the bedpan that Norman Heatly discovered the best and most reliable source for growing penicillin. The war was in full swing and antibiotics were needed in large quantities but a problem finding the best growth medium was proving problematic. He had tested many containers for efficacy in growing the drug, but it would be in the bedpans he borrowed from the Radcliff Infirmary that he would find the greatest success. Because of this unfounded result, he designed a container resembling a bedpan out of ceramic base that would meet their needs. 400 of these stackable pans were made and the demand for penicillin was met (Nobelprize, 2001).

This trail of research then took me to the loo, who knew! It would be from Melbourne that I discovered the greatest volume of documentation. It would be in 1857 that protests and lobbying began in earnest for the establishment of the public loo. There would be restrictions of course, such as they were only for men. J. G. Knight, president of the Victorian Institute of Architects was the greatest advocate for the Public Abolition Room. He classed the development as a measure of moral and sanitary salvation. The original plans drafted in 1857 were for a two-story loo which would have cost over 3000 pounds, a phenomenal amount of money for the day equal to the annual income of 30 gold miners. In 1859 the City Council agreed to build a public urinal for the light sum of 100 pounds. Made of lumbar and iron, its' prime feature was that it was built over a gutter (for sewage purposes) and it allowed a man to hang on to his horse at the same time (Schauble, 1980).

As popularity grew, so did the class of the loo. Lacework iron, gas lamps and multi-seated facilities were some of the beautification works. The creation would soon render its' own problems as a lack of water, buildup of waste and outbreaks of cholera and diphtheria were rampant. It would be another 40 years before the water crisis would be resolved in Melbourne. From 1903 until World War I began there was a boom in the public urinal business. The Aussies took the loo to another level in the development of the underground loo in 1918, which did prove to be only partially successful as water from the road would splash on the innocent occupant below. It is unbelievable to think that no new construction has occurred since the 40's and one must pay a fee to use those still functioning facilities (Schauble, 1980).

So while this search did not take me on the journey I had anticipated, I did discover one international common goal. We all want to capture that which we so desperately wish to eliminate. Whether in a tree, pan, jug or street gutter we will find a way to eliminate it, collect it, carry it and throw it away.

References

Civilization.org (2005). Canadian-Made Ironstone. Retrieved May 7, 2005 from
www.civilization.ca/hist/poterie/po06eng.html

Duncan, I. (1983). Makeshift Medicine: Combating Disease in Japanese Prison Camps. Australian Medical Journal, AU. Retrieved May 20, 2005 from
www.cofepow.org.uk/pages/medical_makeshift_medicine.htm

Nobelprize.org (2001).The Discovery of Penicillin. Retrieved May 1, 2005 from
http://nobelprize.org/medicine/educational/penicillin/readmore.html

Schauble, J. (1980). Monuments in lieu of memories. The Age, AU. Retrieved May 1, 2005 from

http://150.theage.com.au/view_bestofarticle.asp?straction=updat
e&innttype=1&intid=706

von Münch, E., WM. (2011). Technology review of urine diversion components - Overview on urine diversion components such as waterless urinals, urine diversion toilets, urine storage and reuse systems. *Gesellschaft für Internationale Zusammenarbeit (GIZ)* GmbH